Student Procrastination

Palgrave Student to Student

How to Get a First *Michael Tefula*
Student Brain Food *Lauren Lucien*
Student Procrastination *Michael Tefula*
Studying as a Parent *Helen Owton*
University Life *Lauren Lucien*

You may also be interested in the following study titles by Palgrave Macmillan:

14 Days to Exam Success *Lucinda Becker*
Brilliant Writing Tips for Students *Julia Copus*
Cite Them Right (9th edn) *Richard Pears and Graham Shields*
Critical Thinking Skills (2nd edn) *Stella Cottrell*
Dissertations and Project Reports *Stella Cottrell*
The Exam Skills Handbook (2nd edn) *Stella Cottrell*
Getting Critical *Kate Williams*
How to Use Your Reading in Your Essays (2nd edn) *Jeanne Godfrey*
How to Write Better Essays (3rd edn) *Bryan Greetham*
How to Write Your Undergraduate Dissertation *Bryan Greetham*
The Palgrave Student Planner *Stella Cottrell*
Planning Your Essay *Janet Godwin*
Reading and Making Notes *Jeanne Godfrey*
Referencing and Understanding Plagiarism *Kate Williams and Jude Carroll*
Reflective Writing *Kate Williams, Mary Woolliams and Jane Spiro*
Skills for Success (2nd edn) *Stella Cottrell*
Study Skills Connected *Stella Cottrell and Neil Morris*
Success in Academic Writing *Trevor Day*
The Study Skills Handbook (4th edn) *Stella Cottrell*
Time Management *Kate Williams and Michelle Reid*
The Undergraduate Research Handbook *Gina Wisker*

For a complete listing of all titles in our Study Skills range please visit
www.palgrave.com/studyskills

Student Procrastination

Seize the Day and Get More Work Done

Michael Tefula

First published 2014 by
PALGRAVE MACMILLAN
Palgrave Macmillan in the UK is an imprint of Macmillan Publishers Limited, registered in England, company number 785998, of Houndmills, Basingstoke,
Hampshire RG21 6XS.

Palgrave Macmillan in the US is a division of St Martin's Press LLC, 175 Fifth Avenue, New York, NY 10010.

Palgrave Macmillan is the global academic imprint of the above companies and has companies and representatives throughout the world.

Palgrave® and Macmillan® are registered trademarks in the United States, the United Kingdom, Europe and other countries

ISBN: 978–1–137–31245–7

This book is printed on paper suitable for recycling and made from fully managed and sustained forest sources. Logging, pulping and manufacturing processes are expected to conform to the environmental regulations of the country of origin.

A catalogue record for this book is available from the British Library.

A catalog record for this book is available from the Library of Congress.

Printed in China

Contents

Preface

When I was given the opportunity to write a book on student procrastination, I wondered whether I could take up the challenge. After all, I am not a professor of psychology, nor am I someone who never procrastinates. In fact, I struggled with procrastination both at university and in my subsequent professional studies.

With that said, I consider these weaknesses to be strengths too, because I have approached this book from the perspective of someone who frequently has to overcome procrastination, as opposed to someone who has never had an issue with putting things off. So, how did I end up here?

At university, I was faced with the same distractions and temptations all students face but fortunately managed to minimise procrastination to a level that allowed me to graduate with a first. I subsequently had to dig deeper in terms of focus and willpower to write my debut book, *How to Get a First: Insights and Advice from a First-class Graduate*.

Upon graduation, I secured a job to train as a chartered accountant in the world of corporate finance where I was, yet again, faced with a large number of exams and revision to do over the course of my training contract.

To date, I have six years behind me of university and professional studies, and as well as having authored two books, I have had my fair share of project work, deadlines, time pressure, and productivity issues. With this book, I hope some of my experiences, research and insights will save you from the difficulties I faced when trying to get things done!

Introduction

A curious case of procrastination

It's 8.30 a.m. on Tuesday and Emily is trembling with fear. The ensuing panic and bewilderment as to where all her time went, along with the crash that follows the gobbling up of cheap energy drinks, can't be helping.

However, time pressure usually leads to an adrenaline boost and, despite the frenzy, Emily now has a renewed sense of focus and purpose: to bash out and proofread the last 500 words of a 3,000-word essay she has been writing since Monday morning – all within 20 minutes.

The essay is due at 9.00 a.m. on the day. By finishing at 8.50 a.m. Emily will be able to print off the essay, submit a soft copy online, and rush off to the Law School to submit a hard copy.

Fortunately, she makes it in the nick of time and submits the coursework before the deadline. 'This is the last time I will leave things till late,' she tells herself. Strange as it may seem, Emily also got a bit of a buzz from the drama that commenced as a result of leaving things till the last minute.

Perhaps Emily enjoys working under pressure. The last time she submitted coursework this late she got 67 per cent, nearly a first. Or does the 'buzz' of working under pressure only appeal if followed by a big sigh of relief at having managed to successfully meet a deadline? Regardless, things aren't looking so good this time round.

In the final hours of her deadline, Emily lost the 'big picture' in her essay as she raced to submit the work on time. The essay was flimsy, at best, and rushing through it was a disservice to her ability to produce intelligent and creative work. What was she thinking? Ample time was given (a whole four weeks) in which to complete the essay, yet here she was, worrying whether she had done enough to even scrape a pass.

Where did all that time go and what did Emily do in the four weeks prior to the deadline? The answer is all too common: she procrastinated, a lot. What does that have to do with you or me? We can all identify with her.

The epidemic

Student procrastination is rampant at university. Everyone more or less does it and most students readily admit to it being a problem. Just to give you a feel of how bad things are, here are some statistics to consider.

Around 80 to 95 per cent of students procrastinate at some point in their academic lives. More specifically, 50 per cent report that they procrastinate often and problematically (Steel, 2007). With that said, in a survey by researchers Zarick and Stonebraker (2009), it was amusing to see that only one student out of 200 claimed to not suffer from the common pitfalls of procrastination (i.e., lower quality work, late submissions, and lower exam marks).

The above findings suggest that we have what could be considered a problem of 'epidemic proportions' (Balkis, 2013). Nevertheless, we tend to joke about the matter without truly appreciating the possible harm procrastination can do.

For example, in an academic context a large body of research now shows that there is a negative association between procrastination and academic performance (Chow, 2011). Indeed, procrastinators do worse at university as a result of not allowing sufficient time to do what is required of them.

In general life, researchers are finding that procrastinators tend to be more miserable in the long term (Wilson and Nguyen, 2012), perhaps because they procrastinate about other important matters such as health (e.g., losing weight) and finance (e.g., managing a student loan).

In sum, the most typical result of procrastination is underperformance (Dewitte and Schouwenburg, 2002). But given how widespread the epidemic is and how severe the consequences of chronic procrastination can be, it is encouraging to see that a large number of people would like to see it reduced. This is certainly evident given the demand for advice on the topic.

At the time of writing, a Google search of the term 'procrastination' typically returns 4 million hits, while a search on Amazon returns over 1,000 publications on the subject. With so much advice in the area it is hard to know where to start, and sometimes the advice can seem overwhelmingly diverse and unconnected.

My hope with this book is that you will find within it a more coherent approach that can help you understand the causes of procrastination and how you can overcome it and get more work done.

The journey ahead

Procrastination is a complicated psychological and physiological problem. This is part of the reason why there are so many books, articles and other media on the subject. But amongst all this advice it is easy to get lost and lose track of what the underlying problems really are.

Accordingly, the first half of this book will introduce you to what I call the *Four Ps of Procrastination*. These are four categories within which I have placed the most common causes of procrastination behaviour. I hope that such a framework will make it easier for you to identify and remember what could be leading to you delaying your work.

In order, the Four Ps of Procrastination are:

1 Probability of Payoff
2 Pursuit of Pleasure
3 Prevention of Pain
4 Postponement of Punishment (or Payoff)

I will explain each of these categories in later chapters and I would encourage you to take the time to understand them before proceeding to the second half of the book.

In the first part of the book, you will also find Thinking Point and Suggestions boxes. These are there to help you consider the practical implications of some of the research and ideas on procrastination and how you may combat the habit. Make the book your own and scribble notes in the margin if you are inspired by the text to come up with ideas of your own.

In addition to the above, Diagnosis Corners have been placed at the end of each of the chapters of the four Ps. While not exhaustive, the diagnosis questions will help you identify the reason for procrastinating and will also point you in the right direction in terms of remedies.

After the Four Ps of Procrastination you will find a number of big-theme strategies that I have provided as a foundation from which you can learn how to minimise procrastination. I will share ideas on Competence and Confidence, Motivation, Willpower, Focus and Attention, Goals and Planning ('the big 5'), as well as counterintuitive ideas for when all else fails.

On the whole, this book aims to help you understand the causes of student procrastination and follows on by sharing some of the most effective ways of combating the habit.

But note: we all have different personalities and character traits. I cannot guarantee that you will find all the answers you need in this book. However, once you are armed with an understanding of the routes to procrastination, and once you have familiarised yourself with the suggested ideas for overcoming the problem, you will find it easier to come up with your own solutions, which may even be more powerful than those suggested in this title.

What Is Procrastination?

Chapter illustrations by Francisco Maldonado and colouring provided by Oscar Blanco.

Origins and definitions

The verb 'procrastination' has its origins in the sixteenth-century Latin word *procrastinare*. When broken down, *pro* means 'forward' while *crastinus* means 'belonging to tomorrow'. A combination of these two components can vaguely be translated to mean 'moving something forward to tomorrow'. In other words, delaying something.

Most dictionaries follow the above idea when defining procrastination and it is often explained as the act of putting things off to a later date. But such descriptions are fairly general and fail to account for a key distinction, most eloquently highlighted by researcher Dr Timothy Pychyl in his book *Procrastinator's Digest*, where he observes: 'all procrastination is delay, but not all delay is procrastination' (Pychyl, 2010).

The opposite of procrastination

Why the philosophy? It's important to recognise and identify what exactly procrastination is, and is not, before we can tackle it. One way of obtaining such clarity is by considering the opposite.

Funnily enough, when I was first asked what the opposite of procrastination is, I could not come up with an answer. But after some digging I found a close enough solution: the opposite of procrastination may be referred to as being punctual (Dewitte and Schouwenburg, 2002). That is, you are punctual if you submit your work before its deadline just as much as someone is punctual if they arrive on time and don't stand you up.

Do note, however, that being punctual in the general time-keeping sense doesn't mean you are less of a procrastinator with university work. There are students who are good at being on time for social events or even lectures, yet they struggle with procrastination and often delay the completion of their assignments.

Not all delay is procrastination

Delaying your revision until tomorrow does not automatically mean you are procrastinating. You might be really tired (although this is more often a hollow excuse not to work than actual depletion of energy), or you could be waiting for key syllabus information from your lecturer.

Frank Partnoy, an ex-investment banker and author of *Wait: The Art and Science of Delay* (2012), advises that sometimes we are simply better off taking more time to gather and process information before moving ahead. In fact, in Roman times, the term *procrastinare* is argued to have had less negative connotations. For example, the word could be used in situations when an army general found it wiser to be patient and wait the enemy out, instead of rushing into war (Ferrari, Johnson and McCown, 1995).

And so, merely delaying a piece of work does not in itself mean you are procrastinating. There are many good reasons why you may have to put off your work. But be wary of dubious reasons, for if there is one thing we students are good at, it is making up really creative and convincing excuses to avoid work.

What procrastination *is*

In writing this book I scoured academic journals and philosophical literature for a contemporary and precise definition of what procrastination is. While the definitions were abundant, many were riddled with academic terms, anecdotal musings and mind experiments that only provided me with another form of procrastination (I should have been writing more of this book instead of wandering off on a tangential search for precise definitions).

Eventually, I came across the work of Dr Piers Steel, a researcher who is often referred to as the world's leading authority on the science of procrastination. In a meta-analytical review (this is where researchers combine and review results from numerous studies, often running into the hundreds), Dr Steel considered a range of definitions for procrastination and suggested a combination that has stuck with me since:

> To procrastinate is to voluntarily delay an intended course of action *despite expecting to be worse off for the delay*. (Steel, 2007)

Student procrastination

Given the above definition of procrastination, what does it really look like in the student world? Here are a few anecdotes on student procrastination that might ring a bell. (Note, from here on I use the words *procrastination* and *student procrastination* to refer to the same idea of students putting off their work.)

Procrastination is when you tell yourself that another minute of watching YouTube clips won't hurt. And the extra minute after that? Well, it's only a minute extra, right?

Procrastination is when just a little bit more fun, unbeknownst to the student who thinks a few more minutes of play won't hurt, eventually builds up to hours, days and weeks of wasted time with nothing to show for it.

Procrastination is when empty pages of an unwritten essay drive you to wash greasy dishes that have been lying in the sink for weeks; for it seems easier to face fungi-infested cutlery than to start your work.

Procrastination is when we can muster up the courage to tackle absolutely anything, so long as it isn't the work that we should be doing – because, truth be told, it's easier to spend hours meticulously rearranging digital music libraries, social media content, stationery equipment, as well as (and this is rather ironic) plans for the very work that we should be doing, than making progress on university assignments.

Procrastination is when you can't start revising because you don't feel like it. You then tell yourself, day after day, that you will feel more like it tomorrow – a tomorrow that keeps moving closer and closer to your day of reckoning.

Procrastination is when the fridge or snack cupboard becomes a place of constant, where you zombishly nibble on something every five minutes during your study efforts.

Procrastination is when you go to the library with the best of intentions only to leave a few hours later, wondering how it is that you managed to achieve nothing by the end.

Procrastination is a short-term gain being exchanged for long-term pain. More precisely, student procrastination is the act of putting off university work to a later time at the expense of our future self. The principle is always the same: *Play* now, *pay* later, and with lots of interest.

Indeed, student procrastination takes many forms, but, as a student journalist once put it, the ultimate form of the habit boils down to not doing much about what you should be doing, and in the end, having no end product (Burch, 2012).

Snapshot Conclusion

- ☝ Student procrastination is the act of putting off university work, which you know you should be doing sooner rather than later.
- ☝ You can tell you are procrastinating with the help of a simple question:

    Given your academic demands and deadlines, have you started to work on what you know, deep down, you should be doing at this moment in time? If the answer is no, you are most likely procrastinating (unless you are reading this book, of course).

Part 1

The Four Ps of Procrastination

Probability of payoff We would rather do things we are likely to succeed in and where the rewards mean something to us, than things that do not hold these promises.	**Pursuit of pleasure** We naturally have a preference for what is pleasurable and therefore tempting distractions and boredom hamper academic efforts.
Prevention of pain We avoid work that is hard, ambiguous, or too big to start. The more challenging or tedious the work, the more we put it off.	**Postponement of punishment (or payoff)** We find it easier to put things off because the consequences of indulgences today are usually delayed.

Procrastination

The Four Ps of Procrastination are a way of categorising the causes of students unnecessarily putting things off. Knowing which of the four Ps apply in a particular bout of procrastination should help you tailor an appropriate response to combat the affliction. At the end of each of the next four chapters, diagnosis corners will provide hints on areas that may be worth considering in this regard.

1

Probability of Payoff

The Procrastination Connection

Do you lack the necessary skills and confidence in your work? Does making an effort seem meaningless? Or perhaps fear of failure and perfectionism have paralysed you from making a start. Whatever the case, this chapter will help you understand how and why these factors contribute to procrastination.

Whsat are your chances?

Would you bother going to a test if the examiner told you upfront that they were going to fail you? Would you even bother preparing for it? I know I wouldn't. Or how about this: would you ever ask someone out on a date if they told you in advance that they were going to say no? I suspect not.

Our motivation to pursue a goal or to start working on an assignment is usually dependent on whether we think we can achieve that goal or successfully complete that assignment. By the same token, our motivation to work usually depends on how much we value successful completion of a task (Wigfield, 1994).

Researchers in the field of achievement and motivation took note of this notion over 50 years ago (see Atkinson, 1957) and have since been hammering away at understanding the phenomenon better.

To date, one of the key theoretical models that have proved to be reliable in predicting the performance and persistence of students is the expectancy-value model of achievement (Wigfield and Eccles, 2000).

Despite the economics-sounding name, the principles of expectancy-value theory are simple and can be whittled down to two key components that lie within its name – expectancy and value.

Bluntly put, this theory posits that we will only do something if we expect to succeed at it and when this success is valuable or meaningful to us. Remove or lower either of these factors and we end up not acting on a goal or objective.

Inspired by the above comes the first P of procrastination: *probability of payoff*. This element of student procrastination is based on: (1) the expectancy of success (probability), and (2) the worthiness of an outcome (payoff). In the following sections we explore how these factors influence student procrastination and what the main symptoms are in this regard.

Expectancy

Before you start your university work, at some point you will wonder what your chances of success are. Thoughts on your ability to succeed will include internal beliefs about your abilities and external beliefs about the outcome of your actions.

These two notions are sometimes referred to as *efficacy expectations* and *outcome expectations* (Bandura, 1997), and having deficiencies in either can contribute to how much you procrastinate. Let us consider each in a bit more detail.

Efficacy expectations are internal beliefs about your abilities (the word 'efficacy' is just another term for 'having the skill to do something') – for example, how good you think you are at writing essays. Outcome expectations, on the other hand, are external beliefs that your skills and effort will lead to a certain result (Eccles and Wigfield, 2002).

One way of visualising the above contrast is with the following diagram and questions:

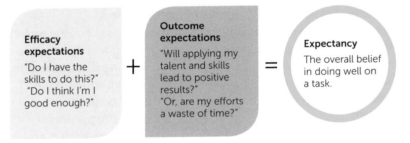

Efficacy expectations

"Do I have the skills to do this?"
"Do I think I'm I good enough?"

+

Outcome expectations

"Will applying my talent and skills lead to positive results?"
"Or, are my efforts a waste of time?"

=

Expectancy

The overall belief in doing well on a task.

When procrastinating, you should look out for which of the two components on the left side of the equation may be holding you back. Indeed, it is entirely possible for you to have great confidence in your abilities (i.e., knowing that you can produce good-quality work), while having little to no confidence in the outcome of your efforts (i.e., doubting that your performance and application of skill will be rewarded).

Likewise, you may know exactly what needs to be done to score really well on an assignment, and know what boxes to tick on the syllabus (high outcome expectation), yet you may procrastinate because you either lack the technical skill to do those things or you doubt your execution will be of a high enough quality to attract high marks.

Therefore, as a student, be wary of the role efficacy and outcome expectancies play in how much you procrastinate. Whether you think you have what it takes to do well, and whether you believe skills and effort are rewarded appropriately, will determine how moved you are to start your work.

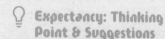

Expectancy: Thinking Point & Suggestions

• If what you believe about your chances of success contributes to procrastination, can you think of ways in which you could reduce the habit by working on your efficacy and outcome expectations?

• Suggested reading: Chapter 5 – Competence and Confidence.

Payoff

The second factor to consider in *probability of payoff* is the payoff itself (or value). After all, why would any student bother working hard to complete an assignment if its results were meaningless?

A good example of the payoff concept at play in the UK is the way the first year of university is structured on some courses. Where it doesn't contribute to the final grade upon graduation, nothing is more tempting than to put off as much work as possible the moment you hear the following words of liberation: 'The first year doesn't count!'

In fact, first-year students on such courses often struggle for motivation when they realise that efforts in the opening year will not contribute to their degree classification. I certainly did not thrive until my second and final years of study, and the reasons are clear: we need to have a strong reason for doing something. Otherwise, we end up not trying at all.

So what type of payoff-related reasons drive effort, the lack of which lead to procrastination? The answer can be found in four key tenets brought to light by psychologists many years ago. These are: (1) attainment value, (2) intrinsic value, (3) cost, and (4) utility value (Eccles et al., 1983). Each of the reasons is explained in turn below.

Attainment value

Attainment value is how important you think it is for you to do well on an assignment. It is also about your needs and personal identity. For example, a student might not care much for grades. Instead, they might consider themselves more creative in nature than academically focused. In this instance, they place a low attainment value in preparing for exams and as a result end up more likely to delay revision, for instance.

Likewise, a music student with a love for playing guitar may find it easier to prepare for a gig than for a graduate job interview in a large corporation. Such a student probably identifies with music more than a 9-to-5 job and would therefore be less motivated to practise interview questions.

In contrast, if you always got good grades in school and you identify yourself as someone that loves to learn, you are more likely to place a high attainment value in doing well at university. For this reason you would be expected to have more motivation in this area, even when faced with setbacks.

Joe Barry, a recent University of Warwick graduate who now works in finance, is a particularly good example of someone who used to do well in school and continues to identify himself with doing well:

> 'I recall submitting my first essay in first year and getting a mark of 52. I went to the lecturer as I was in shock. However, he greeted me as follows: "I bet you were the cleverest in your college right?," to which I begrudgingly responded "Yes, I suppose so".
>
> The lecturer went on to say that everyone at the university was the best at their old college as well and that I was no longer a big fish in a small pond. Regardless, that spurred me on to make myself that big fish again.'

As expected, attainment value is part of the reason why students can be lazy in some parts of their university work while working extremely hard in other areas. On the whole, if the successful completion of a task isn't aligned with who you are, or who you would like to be, you are more likely to procrastinate in completing that task.

Intrinsic value

The next tenet to consider is intrinsic value. This relates to how much you enjoy doing something. It is when the journey – and not necessarily the destination – is the reward. In essence, intrinsic value pertains to the gratification you get from doing something while you are doing it. The process is enjoyed without great emphasis on the outcome.

For example, if you have a driving licence, think back to when you had just passed your driving test. You would look for any opportunity to go out for a drive, not so much to get somewhere, but to enjoy the process of driving itself. That is intrinsic motivation. It is akin to having a passion for something, and in such instances we procrastinate less.

But beware: a number of self-help books and career guides have popularised a shallow version of the concept of passion. Intrinsic motivation is not something you are necessarily born with. Nor is it always something that's already out there but just needs to be found. Sometimes it has to be cultivated (Newport, 2012).

Consider the driving example mentioned earlier. When you start taking driving lessons, it can be tough, frustrating, scary, and no more enjoyable than facing the drudgery of academic work. However, after a few lessons something clicks. You master the basics and attain greater confidence in controlling the vehicle. And it is then that you start to enjoy the process of driving.

University work is no different. When it is challenging, you may not enjoy doing the work initially (i.e., low intrinsic motivation). However, once your skills improve you may find that you genuinely enjoy the work (i.e., higher intrinsic value). With that being said, if the work remains boring or beyond your abilities, procrastination is inevitable.

Cost

The next tenet is cost. Sometimes we delay our work purely because of the time and effort we expect to expend. If you perceive a task to require a large amount of time to complete, you will be more likely to procrastinate, because the work at hand takes time away from activities that could be more immediately enjoyable.

Here is a simple scenario. When faced with a 10,000-word dissertation, would you rather vacuum your room or make a start on the assignment? The natural instinct for most students is to swiftly weigh up which task is quicker and less costly to do, and then engage in that activity.

In some ways, we are creatures of economy and, when faced with work, we would rather opt for the easier and cheaper route.

Utility

The final tenet of value in our work is utility. This raises the question of what completing an assignment can do for you in the short and long term.

For example, you may have come to university to get a degree that will lead to a well-paying graduate job. Or perhaps, more traditionally, you simply enrolled to make your parents proud.

Utility value generally concerns more practical matters and can be roused with some of the following questions:

- ☙ Will this degree improve my life?
- ☙ Will it get me on to a Master's course?
- ☙ Will this module enhance my employment prospects? ... and so on.

All in all, attempting to do work for which you see no practical value can be the final nail in the coffin when it comes to procrastination. Motivation is especially dire when the link between effort and utility is non-existent.

As such, always consider whether you can't be bothered to work because what you are doing doesn't matter.

 Payoff (value): Thinking Point & Suggestions

- **Do you know why you are at university? Have you considered the value of doing well? If not, you will find it particularly hard to get on with your work and may end up procrastinating more often.**

- **Suggested reading: Chapter 6 – Motivation.**

The first P

The *probability of payoff* concept sheds light on where our motivation is sourced. The question of whether one procrastinates or not can be tied to our beliefs in our abilities, the perceived credibility of reward systems, and how valuable the final reward is to us.

Having deficiencies in any of the above areas should be of concern to any student, and, in later chapters, multiple strategies will be offered to remedy some of these areas. But before we get ahead of ourselves, it's worth considering how the *first P of procrastination* (referred to as P-1) manifests itself in other areas.

Manifestations of P-1

Confidence, self-esteem, self-efficacy

Students who lack confidence and self-esteem can be prone to putting off challenging work. However, procrastination research in the area has revealed more than that. We now know that the greater culprit in the matter is low self-efficacy for self-regulation ('SESR'): that is, an individual's beliefs in their ability to use various strategies to learn, resist distractions and complete their work (Klassen, Krawchuk and Rajani, 2008).

How does this differ from self-confidence and self-esteem? Well, self-esteem is about your self-worth and your overall opinion about yourself (NHS, 2013). Self-confidence, on the other hand, is a more general term that refers to the strength of any belief, regardless of whether it is positive or negative (Bandura, 1997).

Moreover, self-efficacy for self-regulation is more specific and changes from task to task. For example, I find reading and editing drafts easier to manage and I am usually less distracted during such a process. My SESR is high in this area.

On the other hand, I used to struggle with writing and generating ideas. My SESR was low in this area and I would procrastinate often. However, once I acquired certain strategies to help with idea generation, writing, and how to focus better, my SESR increased and now I procrastinate less in this area.

Sure, self-confidence and self-esteem can be attributed to procrastination behaviours. However, self-efficacy plays the greater role due to its specificity.

> ### 💡 Confidence/Self-Esteem: Thinking Point & Suggestions
>
> • **General confidence and self-esteem are not enough. To curb the habit of putting off your work it is also important to consider working on the skills necessary to do well on the task you are faced with (i.e., self-efficacy).**
>
> • **Suggested reading: Chapter 5 – Competence and Confidence.**

Fear of failure

Both students and researchers alike often mention the words 'fear of failure' when it comes to discussing procrastination. I have noticed this even more so in the creative industries (e.g., musicians delaying starting work on a project out of a fear that their fans will not like the output) than in the lives of students.

All the same, I initially doubted how commonly 'fear of failure' cropped up as a reason for procrastination at university. After all, why would a student avoid revising out of a fear of failing an exam? Surely the fear of failing that exam would drive one to work even harder? (I know far too many students whose fear of failure has driven them to become over-achievers.)

But fear of failure is indeed a legitimate concern. A number of the university students I spoke to when writing this book did share worries about their work being judged negatively, and how this sometimes resulted in anxieties around starting their assignments. It is not uncommon for many of us to limit our efforts, because we would rather be judged as procrastinators than be criticised on the work we put our best efforts into.

Given the above, it is surprising to note that correlational studies (studies which seek to understand the link between two things) have shown that a fear of failure is only weakly (or non-significantly) related to procrastination (Haghbin, McCaffrey and Pychyl, 2012). This initially suggests that either fear of failure doesn't matter that much or the relationship it has with procrastination is more complicated.

The answer, it turns out, is somewhat self-evident. In a paper titled 'The complexity of the relation between fear of failure and procrastination', Dr Pychyl and his colleagues demonstrated that the effects fear of failure has on procrastination are actually moderated by how competent people feel they are.

That is, students who consider themselves highly competent (high self-efficacy) are more likely to start and finish their work on time to avoid the consequences and pain of failing (for example, over-achievers can be positively motivated by a fear of failure).

On the other hand, students who believe they have low competence (low self-efficacy) are more likely to procrastinate when a fear of failure is present. Such students are more easily distracted by irrelevant activities as the anxiety of facing their work is at times too much to bear.

> **Fear of failure: Thinking Point & Suggestions**
>
> • Being overly concerned with what other people think can paralyse you from taking action. More frequently, however, being incompetent at something makes the fear of failure more salient and paralysing. Can you think of ways to overcome this?
>
> • Suggested reading: Chapter 5 – Competence and Confidence (pp. 63–6).

In any case, fear of failure influences procrastination behaviour to varying extents. In particular, when it is coupled with low competence, it can be especially detrimental to our ability to complete work assigned to us on time.

Perfectionism

Another common reason for procrastination among students is that of perfectionism, which can also be linked to a fear of failure. Examples of perfectionist tendencies include:

- excessive research;
- overindulgent planning;
- obsessive editing, and so forth.

Nevertheless, at least in the above instances some progress is being made. I, for one, spent far too long reading about procrastination; however, it did still contribute to my knowledge in the area despite eating into the time it would take to write this book.

More severe cases of perfectionism concern students being paralysed by unrealistic standards, set either by themselves or someone else. As such, they delay the work as much as they can to avoid the pain they would face for not meeting such standards.

But, like fear of failure, I know some students who consider themselves perfectionists and yet they are the last I would ever consider to be procrastinators. These students set high standards for themselves but, somehow, like athletes who train meticulously to perfect a swing or jump, use perfectionism to their advantage: they thrive, precisely because of their perfectionist tendencies.

Why the difference? Yet again, turning to procrastination research can enlighten us. Studies involving tens of thousands of subjects have shown that perfectionism alone has no significant influence on procrastination (Steel, 2012). However, this doesn't rule out the potential for other mediating factors (as was the case with fear of failure).

Clearly, there is a harmful side and a useful side to perfectionism and this has led to psychologists distinguishing the two sides as follows:

Maladaptive perfectionism (the harmful version)
Maladaptive perfectionists worry about what others will think of them if they fail to succeed. They take failures and mistakes personally, and that often leads to lower self-esteem.

Maladaptive perfectionists also place too much emphasis on *perfect* and their self-worth often depends on it. These are the type of perfectionists who procrastinate a lot (Blackler, 2011).

Adaptive perfectionism (the healthy version)
Adaptive perfectionists, on the other hand, are driven less by what other people think of them and are in it for the learning and mastery of

a subject. They do not base their self-worth on perfect execution, but rather, on the results of hard work.

These perfectionists are the ones who tend to engage less frequently in procrastination (Yao, 2009).

In sum, perfectionism can drive you to work harder. However, it can be damaging if your self-worth is dependent on meeting unrealistic aims. Furthermore, trying to attain 'perfect' may take up far too much time and lead to you not completing your work in a timely fashion.

Perfectionism: Thinking Point & Suggestions

• Striving for perfection can be a form of procrastination because there is no end to that road. However, being comfortable with 'good enough' may serve you better. Can you think of any other ways to overcome the malady?

• Suggested reading: Chapter 5 – Competence and Confidence (pp. 63–6).

Snapshot Conclusion

↪ First, if you do not believe in your ability to do well on a piece of work, you will be more likely to procrastinate.

↪ Second, if the successful completion of an assignment and the rewards that come with it have no personal relevance, the chances of delaying your work increase.

↪ Third, fear of failure can lead to more procrastination, but mostly in instances where we do not believe we have the adequate skills for success.

↪ And finally, if your self-worth is based on doing your work perfectly, you will be more likely to put things off.

Probability of Payoff: P-1 Diagnosis Corner

Are you procrastinating for any of the following reasons?

- **Lacking in competence or confidence** – Are you doubtful of your ability to successfully complete the academic task at hand?
  - See Chapter 5 for possible remedies.
- **Personality and course mismatch** – Does your work seem meaningless? Is it boring? Would you rather be doing something else?
  - See Chapter 6 for possible remedies, in particular, the section on utility on pages 70–2.
- **A fear of failure or maladaptive perfectionism** – Are you worried that you will not do well in your work? Are you placing unrealistic expectations on yourself?
  - See Chapter 5 for possible remedies, especially pages 63–6.

2

Pursuit of Pleasure

The Procrastination Connection

We are hardwired to take more interest in immediate gratification.
The more impulsive we are, the more we give in to such temptations.
Boredom also plays a role and makes it harder for to us persist in our
academic efforts. This chapter considers these issues and how they are
linked to procrastination.

Acting on impulse

Coming to higher education is an exciting right of passage with newfound freedoms. Without your parents to dictate how long you can stay out for, or teachers to chase you up on unfinished homework, university blasts open the gates of autonomy like no other life transition ever will.

However, the price you pay for this freedom is no matter for celebration. And I am not talking about the high university fees. I am talking about the number of distractions and temptations you will face in your academic life.

With so much going on at university, often the procrastination problem isn't just about starting your work; it's also about staying on track once that work commences.

In the previous chapter we saw how belief in your abilities helped or hindered the initiation of work on a given task. But now we turn to a behaviour that affects those students who may have the ability to start their work, but find it hard to finish it: impulsivity.

There are numerous varieties of impulsivity (Evenden, 1999) and psychologists are not short on definitions for it. Nevertheless, we will keep things simple for now and focus on the negative form, which can be defined in the academic context as follows:

> Impulsiveness is the tendency to give in to desires and urges that distract you from your work.

Impulsive behaviour is a serious business. As one researcher put it, 'impulsiveness shares the strongest bond with procrastination' (Steel, 2012). Unfortunately our brains are partly hardwired to act on impulses. The hunter-gatherer section of the brain has a preference for what is immediate and certain, as opposed to what is distant and uncertain (Wilson and Nguyen, 2012).

So, when we pursue short-term pleasures instead of larger rewards that are distant, it is, in some sense, nature taking its course. Still, the less we are able to resist such urges the more we are distracted from our work and the more we procrastinate in completing it. The second P of procrastination, *pursuit of pleasure*, revolves around the above ideas.

Accordingly, in the following sections we will seek to get a better understanding of impulsive behaviour and its link to procrastination. In particular, we will explore four personality routes to impulsiveness suggested by psychologists Stephen Whiteside and Donald Lynam (2001), in the decade's most cited academic article on personality psychology (Allik, 2012). Following that, we will consider links to boredom and also explore a manifestation of these ideas in student life.

A lack of foresight

The first aspect that can lead us to pursue small pleasures now, over greater rewards later, is the fact that there are times when we do not give much thought to the consequences of our actions. Without carefully reflecting on the ramifications of doing something, we place ourselves at the mercy of impulsiveness.

In such instances, going on YouTube to check out one cat video can easily turn into a YouTube marathon session that lasts for hours. You then regret it and wonder where all the time went. But had you considered the fact that YouTube is engineered to keep you watching for as long as possible (the related video links on the side bar are extremely good at doing this), you might have avoided going online in the first instance.

Premeditation, or thinking about something before you do it, is therefore important when it comes to matters of self-control. And nowhere is this emphasis more starkly demonstrated than in modern legal systems.

For example, premeditated crimes lead to harsher sentences than unintended crimes. This is because society believes that when someone engages in a criminal act, all the while knowing the legal consequences, they should also have enough personal control to avoid the criminal act altogether (Morewedge et al., 2009). In other words, if you really think about something before doing it, you should be able to make a better decision.

Similarly, we are weakest in moments where we do not take the time to reflect on the possible outcomes of our decisions. In fact, psychologists have found strong links between a lack of premeditation and harmful behaviours such as eating problems, aggression, and attention deficit disorder (Miller et al., 2003).

Without much foresight, the little pleasures that tempt us can sway us from our work without a conscious consideration of what is best for us – that is, to stick to the task at hand. Furthermore, if we procrastinate about our work in this fashion, all the while knowing the severe consequences of doing so, like the perpetrator of the premeditated crime we usually end up receiving a much harsher sentence – increased self-blame (Morewedge et al., 2009).

 Foresight: Thinking Point & Suggestions

• Next time you are faced with a guilty pleasure that could sway you from your work, take a couple of seconds to consider its ramifications. You may find that with a bit of foresight, certain temptations lose their appeal.

• Suggested reading: Chapter 7 – Willpower / Chapter 8 – Focus and Attention.

In the heat of the moment

The second route to impulsive behaviour is what I like to refer to as acting in the heat of the moment. It is when you feel strong urges to do something impulsive when under conditions of pressure, stress or depression. It is at times such as these that you feel more inclined to indulge in a bit of pleasure now in the hope of alleviating negative feelings.

Have you ever found yourself repeatedly heading for the fridge to snack during a revision session and all the while your books remain unopened? That is an example of acting in the heat of the moment and it can be quite distracting when it comes to successfully finishing a piece of work. With that said, there is much to learn form the underlying physiological process of such behaviours.

When experiencing negative emotions, our body changes in interesting ways. For one, stress brings about the increased production of the 'stress hormone', cortisol (Putman et al., 2010). While cortisol is a useful chemical (it is typically associated with fight or flight responses, where it helps increase glucose levels to provide energy for muscles), too much of it can be harmful (Aronson, 2009).

In fact, cortisol has been shown to lead to wounds healing at a slower rate (Ebrecht et al., 2004). And, more worryingly, research suggests that increased cortisol exposure may weaken the part of the brain that is associated with self-control, proper planning and decision making (Adam and Epel, 2007).

By way of example, one study found that women on diets end up eating more junk food when under stress (Zellner et al., 2006). And in another, male subjects with increased cortisol levels were more likely to engage in high-risk bets for more immediate rewards (Van den Bos, Harteveld and Stoop, 2009).

Clearly, stress can have an impact on self-control and willpower, muscles you certainly do not want to do without in combating procrastination. Yet student life is full of stressors. And whether they are academic or not, evidence suggests they may contribute to impulsiveness.

As such, when you are faced with tedious university work, and you are stressed and fed up, be aware that your sensitivity to act on a whim for immediate gratification is likely to be higher.

 In the heat of the moment: Thinking Point & Suggestions

- If stress has an impact on how likely we are to give in to distracting temptations, are there any ways you could think of to minimise stress in your academic life?

- Suggested reading: Chapter 5 – Competence and Confidence (pp. 62–3).

Adrenaline junkie (sensation seeking)

The third route to impulsive behaviour is sensation seeking. This facet of personality is especially acute in individuals who are adrenaline junkies. (Here, I use the term *adrenaline junkie* loosely to refer to people who like exciting activities and are usually open to trying new experiences.) These are people who will try most things at least once, regardless of risk (Whiteside and Lynam, 2001).

Simply put, sensation seekers prefer novelty to tradition, and having this type of personality means you are more likely to be distracted from your work the moment a shiny experience or thing pops up (much like the poor girl in the opening illustration to this chapter).

Note, however, that adrenaline junkies do not necessarily seek risk for risk's sake. Stimulation can still be achieved via other, safer options such as exotic travel, avant-garde art, exciting media and high-impact sports (Roberti, 2004). The problem is, academic life doesn't always provide such thrills, and if you are a student who requires high stimulation, it can prove difficult to stay focused and engaged with work that does not live up to other forms of excitement.

On the other hand, unlike people who are sensitive to stressful situations and are more likely to falter in the heat of the moment, sensation-seeking people are somewhat numb to acute stress. And studies corroborate this: it has been shown that sensation seekers have a 'blunted cortisol release' in response to stress (Roberti, 2004). That is, someone who loves skydiving may not respond to a high-pressure deadline in the same way that someone who is scared of rollercoasters would.

Clearly, there are possible benefits to being an adrenaline junkie – namely, being more accommodating to stress. Nevertheless, staying engaged with work that doesn't provide the same thrills as other high-octane activities can be especially challenging. And without engagement, procrastination is likely.

 Adrenaline junkie: Thinking Point & Suggestions

- **Personalities with a preference for sensation seeking may find certain academic work dull and therefore procrastinate more about its completion. However, if you can think of ways to make your work more engaging, you can certainly ward off procrastination tendencies.**

- **Suggested reading: Chapter 6 – Motivation.**

Perseverance

Married couples swear the oath, 'till death do us part'. It is a shame we cannot always commit to our work in the same manner. But who can blame you? Staying focused on a task can be extremely hard given that the temptations in student life are never ending.

A house party next door, the Internet, an unlimited supply of student gossip – all these things have the power to pull you away from academic efforts. But not if you have the ability to persevere through your work. Not if you have what psychologist Angela Duckworth refers to as *grit* – the ability to relentlessly work on challenging tasks, all the while maintaining great effort and interest.

We are all already familiar with the concept of grit. We see it in successful students, bankers, painters, lawyers and doctors, all of whom rely on it to excel in their endeavours. But did you know that grit appears to be more predictive of success than IQ? That is what Duckworth and her colleagues learnt in a 2007 study (Duckworth et al., 2007).

Once they put their minds to it, successful people seem to have the ability to see things through to the end. Moreover, some say that 'persistence is the other side of the creativity coin' (Adelson, 2003). It is therefore no surprise that people who persevere are not only the ones that finish what they start, but also the ones that often come up with great ideas.

In sum, the concept of perseverance (or grit) is linked to self-control and willpower. Without either of these, you will find it hard to resist the lure of pleasures competing for your attention and will struggle to finish your work.

 Perseverance: Thinking Point & Suggestions

• Seeing something through to the end and persevering in the face of challenging work requires a good amount of willpower to fend off procrastination. Can you think of ways to build self-control, willpower and focus?

• Suggested reading: Chapter 7 – Willpower / Chapter 8 – Focus and Attention.

Boredom

In my first year of university I remember being given lists of academic journals to read as homework. However, my attempts at reading them usually faltered the moment I got to the main body of the text. My mind would wander, I would get bored, and eventually I would put off reading the article until later. Imagine that: someone who loves to read and write procrastinating about reading!

Nonetheless, it seems I am not alone in this. Many students – as much as 30 per cent, according to one study (Solomon and Rothblum, 1984) – nearly always or always procrastinate on assigned readings. Some of the students I interviewed while writing this book also shared similar concerns, and in all cases, the common theme was boredom or work that was not interesting.

Emma Louise Prior, a student at the University of Warwick who is pursuing a postgraduate certificate in education had this to say:

> 'Personally I believe that I procrastinate when I am not interested in a task. For example, when completing assignments at university I tend to procrastinate when I do not find the content stimulating. If I do not particularly enjoy the topic I am researching then I will always put off completing the assignment until the last minute.'

Moreover, the idea of being bored has more to it than meets the eye. In some studies, boredom has been linked to numerous impulse control problems (Eastwood et al., 2012). And so it seems that we not only procrastinate when presented with difficult work (more on this in Chapter 3) but also – and especially – when that work is boring (Blunt and Pychyl, 2000). For instance, a task as simple as filling in a questionnaire can be procrastinated over just as much as the requirement to write a 10,000-word dissertation.

With that said, it is worth noting that boredom can affect all stages of work, from the planning stage all the way up to the final stages. Indeed boredom can hit at any point and when it does, it weakens our ability to resist other pleasurable, but academically harmful, activities. Luckily for us, there are a number of boredom researchers (no pun intended) who have provided invaluable insights on the topic, namely, its unique relationship with attention (Eastwood et al., 2012). The following six ideas provide insights in this regard.

Unidentified distractions

First, it has been found that when our attention is disrupted, our perception of how boring something is changes. The following experiment is exemplar of this phenomenon.

In the study, participants were asked to listen to someone reading an article and to rate how bored they were in listening to it. One group had a loud TV playing unrelated content next door, another had it at moderate volume (to the extent that it was barely noticeable), and the final group had silence. Which of these groups do you think experienced the greatest boredom?

Group 1
• Loud TV next door

Group 2
• Moderate volume TV next door
• Barely noticeable

Group 3
• Complete silence

Surprisingly, it turned out that the group with the barely noticeable TV sound reported the greatest boredom (Group 2 in the diagram), almost twice as much when compared to the loud and silent conditions. But what was the cause of this?

The conductors of the experiment argued that when the test subjects found it hard to pay attention but could not figure out why, instead of attributing the inattention to the TV (as may have been the case in the loud TV volume group), they had no alternative but to convince themselves that they were finding it hard to concentrate because the material was boring (Damrad-Frye and Laird, 1989).

In other words, when we can't concentrate and are unable to determine the reason we lack focus, we are more likely to report being bored with the material at hand.

> ### ⚲ Unidentified distractions: Thinking Point & Suggestions
>
> • Are you able to identify sources of distraction in your environment? Or perhaps there is something on your mind that keeps bugging you? Eliminating either may help you regain focus, avert boredom and procrastinate less.
>
> • Suggested reading: Chapter 8 – Focus and Attention (pp. 88–90).

Daydreaming

Second, when our mind wanders away from the task at hand to fantasies that are more desirable, our work begins to look paler in comparison (Eastwood et al., 2012). Daydreaming about a holiday on a tropical island provides great contrast to challenging academic work. Indeed, such daydreaming just makes you rate the academic work you are doing as even more boring than it really is.

Innately dull work

Third, sometimes being bored simply comes down to the task itself (i.e., innately boring work). Administrative tasks such as signing forms and completing questionnaires are a good example of this. In such cases, the work just doesn't have much in the way of providing sufficient stimulation. Therefore, we are quick to lose interest, and staying attentive and focused can be especially tough.

Poor information processing

Fourth, when we do not focus on our work enough (i.e., keep giving in to distractions), the inevitable happens. Without sufficient attention, we process information poorly and make more errors. In one sense, we fail a lot more. Nevertheless, instead of blaming our disruptive selves we blame the work and say that it is not interesting. Yet were we to focus intensely on revising, for example, we might grasp ideas and concepts better, have more engagement and ultimately rate the work to be more fascinating.

A lack of autonomy

The fifth scenario is best exemplified by a short anecdote involving a cunning six-year-old named Calvin, and his tiger friend, Hobbes. In an edition of the popular comic strip *Calvin and Hobbes*, the young boy is tasked by his mother to make his bed; something most kids find boring and tedious. With that in mind, Calvin proceeds to gather large pieces of paper and he asks Hobbes to gather some pencils.

Confused, Hobbes asks, 'I thought we were making the bed?' Calvin quickly makes his thoughts clear, 'And do all that work? No, we're going to invent a robot to make the bed for us.' But Hobbes is still puzzled: 'Won't inventing a robot be more work than making the bed?' Not according to Calvin. In all his six years of wisdom the young boy answers back, 'It's only work if someone makes you do it!'

This little six-year-old has it spot on, and researchers of employee attitudes and work behaviour agree. Indeed, when work is clearly imposed on us, there is less of a need to conclude that we are doing it because we are interested it. After all, why would the powers that be impose it upon us if we were already motivated to do it? (An example is when parents pressure students onto certain courses.)

Dr Cynthia Fisher, a professor of management at Australia's Bond University, clarified this point further when she argued that the more blatant and obvious these controls are, the less likely we are to notice the interesting and stimulating bits of an activity. This, in turn, leads to our attention being diverted to other seemingly more interesting things. This then leads to us rating the work we should be doing as more boring (Fisher, 1993).

> ## 💡 Autonomy: Thinking Point & Suggestions
>
> • At university, you are assigned work that you have to do, even when you do not want to do it. However, even when this work is imposed on you, there are ways of making it your own that can help keep you motivated. Can you think of how this can be achieved?
>
> • Suggested reading: Chapter 8 – Focus and Attention (p. 90).

Time drags

Finally, the way we perceive the movement of time appears to influence our perception of boredom. A remarkable study in the 1970s is an example of this idea.

In the study, two groups of students were given a task that objectively lasted for 20 minutes. In one group, a clearly visible clock was rigged to move more slowly, such that the task, according to the fake clock, appeared to last for just 10 minutes. In the second group, the clock was rigged to move much faster, such that, according to the fake clock, the task appeared to last for 30 minutes.

Group 1: Slow clock

Clock rigged to move slower such that 20 minutes looks like 10 minutes

Group 2: Fast cock

Clock rigged to move faster such that 20 minutes looks like 30 minutes

Can you guess which group reported being more bored? Interestingly, it turns out that the students whose clock was rigged to move slower reported being more bored than the group whose clock was rigged to move faster. That is, the students in the first group felt a lot of time had passed (i.e., the objective 20-minute duration of the task), yet when they looked at the clock only 10 minutes had passed. To them, time was literally dragging. The above experiment suggests that when we perceive time to move more slowly, we are likely to report more boredom (London and Monello, 1974).

Moreover, psychologists argue that the way we perceive time actually comes down to our attention and focus. Normally, we perceive the passage of time via 'temporal cues', such as the hands of a clock (as was the case in the above experiment) or changes in lighting (Eastwood et al., 2012).

However, when we are absorbed in interesting work, we tend to ignore these cues and check them less frequently. This, of course, means that when we look at these cues again, larger blocks of time have passed. In one sense, time flies when you are having fun because you check the time less frequently. Conversely, time drags the more you check it, and it is in these instances that our work may appear to be less engaging.

All in all, we rate work to be boring especially when:

⮑ there are distractions we are unable to identify;

⮑ we daydream;

⮑ the work is particularly cumbersome;

⮑ we do not pay sufficient attention to avoid errors;

⮑ we feel that the work is forced upon us; and

⮑ we constantly watch the clock.

And, with boredom, comes the increased likelihood to procrastinate.

 Boredom: Thinking Point & Suggestions

• Boredom is a reason many students cite for not seeing their work through to the end. With a better understanding of boredom, are you able to come up with some ways in which you can make your mind less prone to it?

• Suggested reading: Chapter 8 – Focus and Attention (pp. 88–90).

The second P

The *pursuit of pleasure* highlights why, despite starting our work, we end up taking much longer to finish it. More precisely, we are likely to give in to impulsive desires when we lack foresight, when we are under stress, when we have a thrill-seeking personality or, simply put, when we lack perseverance and engagement.

The *second P of procrastination* (referred to as P-2) is therefore most commonly associated with a combination of tempting distractions that prevent us from sticking to what we started and work that is not engaging enough for us to see it completed punctually. Let us now look at a vivid example of these aspects of procrastination in action.

Manifestations of P-2

Disruption spirals

Your time at university will include some of the best years of your life, probably because you have more freedom and can never run out of fun things to do. Even so, the danger is that all this fun can have adverse multiplicative effects. That is, one distraction from your work can very easily lead to another, and another, until you are left wondering how things got so out of hand. Consider the following example.

You are pumped and ready to start revision for an exam. You decide to get all the course material together to begin your studies and, just as you open the first page of a textbook, your mobile phone vibrates, along with the sound of a social media notification.

Immediately, your body experiences an increase in dopamine, the chemical associated with the brain's reward system. Remarkably, the anticipation alone is enough to spark this chemical change (Sapolsky, 2011) and you immediately feel a bit of excitement. At this stage your mind is already off the books, as you speculate what the message could be or who it's from.

You unlock your phone to see the message: it's a friend's photo album in which you have been tagged. You quickly browse through the pictures you were tagged in and then proceed to check out the other 50 or so pictures from the night before.

It is said that 47 per cent of the time spent online is spent procrastinating (Pychyl and Lavoie, 2001), and so as you browse away unproductively, you only continue to add to the legitimacy of such statistics.

An hour later, you are reading a gossip blog; and many hours later, you are catching up on a favourite show on Netflix. Finally, the day ends and you realise you haven't done any revision whatsoever (even though the nagging thought, 'I should be studying, I should be studying' did not escape you).

If you go back to the start of this spiral we can see that you were unable to resist the urge to check your phone and could not persevere through the first few minutes of studying without giving in to interruptions. One distraction led to another, and by the end of it all you achieved nothing. This is a typical case of what I refer to as disruption spirals (inspired by Dr Steel's (2012), near opposite, success spirals).

Disruption spirals: Thinking Point & Suggestions

• Are you able to identify the early stages of a disruption spiral? This self-awareness can go a long way in helping you to act early, not get sucked into time-wasting antics, and get back to your work.

• Suggested reading: Chapter 8 – Focus and Attention.

Disruption spirals are a commonplace in student life. There are so many little diversions that seem insignificant when taken in isolation, yet they can amount to a whole heap of wasted time when put together. So, before you click that related link, beware of disruption spirals and how much procrastination they can amount to!

Snapshot Conclusion

↻ First, if you do not consider the consequences of the little temptations you give into, you place yourself at risk of disruption spirals that lead to delayed work.

↻ Second, when we are under stress and pressure, our self-control may weaken. In these moments, giving in to temptations becomes easier and more lucrative than getting on with our work.

↻ Third, completing work is effectively akin to a marathon rather than a sprint. Research shows that perseverance is crucial for success, and so without the stamina to bear the challenges of a task, we are unlikely to ever see our work through to completion.

↻ Finally, be aware that not being able to pinpoint sources of distraction, daydreaming and feeling forced to do something makes us rate a task to be more boring than it really is. And in these instances, we are more likely to procrastinate about that task.

Pursuit of Pleasure: P-2 Diagnosis Corner

Are you procrastinating for any of the following reasons?

- **Not seeing the big picture** – Are you failing to consider the larger payoff in the future?
  - See Chapter 6 for remedies.
- **Poor self-control** – Are you struggling to persevere through your work? Are distractions too tempting? Does difficult work leave you especially prone to giving in to the lures of pleasure?
  - See Chapter 7, especially pages 76–81, and Chapter 8 for remedies.
- **Bored and inattentive** – Are you finding your work especially boring and are unable to just get on with it?
  - See Chapter 8, in particular the section on boredom on pages 88–90.

3

Prevention of Pain

The Procrastination Connection

Have you ever felt so overwhelmed by the work ahead that you took solace in putting it off for as long as possible, even if this meant you would have less time and more pressure to do it? This chapter explores this notion and why we procrastinate so much when faced with new and challenging academic work.

Aversion

In which areas of university are you most likely to procrastinate? Attending lectures? Completing your student loan forms? Meeting your society duties? Setting up an event page for a party on Facebook? These are all reasonable contenders; however, they do not top the list of things students procrastinate the most about.

According to researchers, the top three areas of procrastination, as reported by students and in order of severity, are:

1 Writing term papers (for example, essays and other coursework).
2 Studying for exams.
3 Working on weekly assignments.

More than 50 per cent of students endorse these as their main areas of procrastination (Kachgal, Hansen and Nutter, 2001), and the list is unlikely to change in future years (a survey in 1984 by researchers Solomon and Rothblum had the same top-three items). Why? Because these things are tough.

Moreover, the above three areas could be considered the most important in achieving academic success. If you don't finish your coursework, don't keep up with weekly assignments and don't revise for exams, you are unlikely to graduate. But regrettably, they are also areas where students procrastinate the most. Fortunately, in the survey mentioned above, over 60 per cent of students also reported that these were areas where they would most like to reduce their procrastination.

In light of the above, there is a large consensus amongst students and the wider population that when things are perceived to be difficult, especially when compared to easier and more pleasurable tasks, procrastination is likely to occur.

In fact, putting off such tasks makes us feel good, at least in the short term. The third P of procrastination, *prevention of pain*, therefore concerns our tendency to avoid doing things that are challenging, confusing, overwhelming or, in simpler terms, things that are just too painful to do. In this chapter we will explore the specifics of this notion.

Ambiguous (or abstract) work

First, work that is not clear or easy to understand brings about a mixture of unpleasant feelings. Frustration, confusion and repetitive head scratching are not uncommon. All these emotions are unpleasant and, as hinted at before, when we are faced with pain, the natural reaction is to retreat and avoid whatever the cause of pain is.

The following studies, carried out by researchers from universities as far apart as Israel, Germany and New York, are particularly illustrative of the negative effects of assignments that just don't make sense.

In the first illustrative study, Sean McCrea and his colleagues (2008) assigned students a questionnaire for homework, with a set deadline. Questions were randomly assigned to students, with the key difference being the level of ambiguity.

One group received questions framed ambiguously, for example: 'What traits are implied by opening a bank account?' Another group received more 'concrete' questions such as: 'How does one go about opening a bank account?'

Think about the questions above. Which question would you find yourself answering more promptly? The results of the study were not surprising. Students who received the more concrete questions submitted their answers more quickly than those who received the ambiguous question. In fact, 45 per cent more students submitted their answers before the deadline in the concrete group than students who received the vague question (McCrea et al., 2008).

You could argue that the abstract question was 'harder', or that it required more thought, and therefore students took longer to answer it and, in some instances, procrastinated more. Strangely enough, it is possible for the above effects to be noticeable even when the same question is asked of students in both the abstract and concrete groups.

In another study, the same researchers split a different set of students into two groups via priming. This is a psychological process where our behaviour is subliminally influenced by external cues. In the study, while both groups were presented with the same questions, the cover sheets of the questionnaire packs were different (this was the primer).

One group (the abstract group) had a cover sheet with a large picture and the title 'Art and Color: A General Overview'. Another group (the concrete group) had a cover sheet with a more detailed and close-up version of the same picture, but this time, with the title 'Art and Color: A Detailed Examination'.

While both groups had the same questions inside the questionnaire, students responded differently as a result of the difference in priming. More students in the concrete group submitted their answers on time. In contrast, a larger number of students in the abstract group did not even bother returning their questionnaires.

In brief, what these studies tell us is that if work is structured in a vague way, we are more likely to procrastinate about doing it. More surprisingly, how that work is framed also influences our likelihood of completing it on time.

In either case, psychologists theorise that we view abstract tasks as being more distant into the future, and as a result tend not to have a sense of urgency in doing them (McCrea et al., 2008).

> 💡 **Ambigious work: Thinking Point & Suggestions**
>
> • **Academic work can at times be very open ended and, with all the choice about how you can approach an assignment, it is easy to feel paralysed. But there are ways around this. The study above highlights possible solutions. Are you able to think up what these may be?**
>
> • **Suggested reading: Chapter 9 – Goals and Planning (pp. 93–4).**

Antecedent bias

Second, our perception of how unpleasant work might be is also coloured by the activities we do while procrastinating and prior to actually engaging the work. These antecedent activities set a benchmark for pleasantness and our imagination is then left to run wild in speculation as to how unpleasant academic work will be when we come to do it.

A vivid and related example is when you go to see a doctor. Everything seems rosy until they conclude that an injection will be required to complete the diagnosis or treatment. Now, if you are like me, the mere thought of an injection tends to strike fear into the heart that is significantly disproportionate to the pain in reality. Indeed, once the syringe is inserted into the skin the pain isn't anywhere near as bad as our imagination makes it out to be. The same can be said of university work.

A study by researchers at Carleton University, Canada, noticed a phenomenon similar to the above when they tracked the daily activities of students who had an upcoming coursework deadline or exam.

When the students were engaged in something fun, such as playing games or watching television, in these moments they reported that studying would be significantly more unpleasant, difficult and confusing than the fun activities they were doing at the time.

But when students were engaged in studying (an activity they had been procrastinating about earlier), the ratings changed. The odious task of studying now had a significantly lower rating of unpleasantness, difficulty and confusion than previously anticipated (Pychyl et al., 2000).

On the whole, our perception of how difficult something will be tends not to match reality. If we are used to more pleasant things, we often overestimate how unpleasant a task will be and are therefore driven to avoid it more than we really should.

 Antecedent bias: Thinking Point & Suggestions

- Placing your hand from cold water to warm water makes the water feel hotter than it objectively is. The same applies to university work. If you are relaxing, the prospect of doing any work seems worse than it really is. How do you think this inertia can be overcome in order to minimise procrastination?

- Suggested reading: Chapter 7 – Willpower (pp. 80–1).

A lack of skill

Finally, a task is likely to be considered painful if you do not know how to do it. For example, a student who has used the Harvard referencing system many times over will not find the task of using it particularly laborious. But if someone has never used such a system before, they will be more inclined to delay it because they have to go through a substantial amount of effort to find out how it works and how to implement it in their work.

This point is certainly not surprising and there will be some readers thinking, 'Duh?' However, it is worth raising because when we procrastinate, there are many causes at any one time and it is easy to miss some of the more obvious ones. It is not unusual, for example, to find students who feel apathy towards a piece of work but in the midst of distractions and impulsive behaviour, they are unable to identify exactly why they feel this way.

So take heed: if a task appears to be beyond your abilities, there is always a risk of being paralysed by lack of knowledge about how to proceed, as well as being stumped by other emotional maladies like fear of failure (Haghbin et al., 2012).

The third P

The *third P of procrastination* (referred to as P-3) concerns our knee-jerk reaction to painful work: that is, to avoid it at all costs. While painful work is not always synonymous with difficult work (for example, we can be more motivated to complete challenging tasks over easy ones), assignments that are ambiguous, novel and for which we do not have the necessary skills are more likely to lead to procrastination because they bring about a number of unpleasant emotions – namely, confusion, frustration, and being overwhelmed.

As P-3 is inherent in academic work, it is especially important to have an awareness of the ways it manifests itself in a university context; examples are provided to this effect below.

Manifestations of P-3

Too big to start

University work can seem daunting, particularly when looked at as a whole. Writing a 7,000-word essay, preparing for a lengthy set of exams in the final term of university, trying to prepare revision notes when you haven't attended lectures for the last month, all seem insurmountable when tackled in aggregate.

Indeed, there are many instances where the size of an assignment alone is enough to intimidate even the most motivated students from starting their work. Think your 7,000-word final year dissertation is tough? Well, how about 50,000– 100,000 words – the typical length of a PhD thesis? The thought alone makes me want to procrastinate, as that would surely be more pleasant than writing such a lengthy piece. Where on earth do you even start in crafting a 100,000-word document?

With that said, despite being older, and perhaps even more motivated, doctoral students are not immune from being overwhelmed by the task and, as one professor noted, this is perhaps the most common reason for PhD students to procrastinate about their PhD work (Kuther, 1999).

Amusingly, the pain that doctoral students go through in writing their theses is so severe that one PhD student, Jorge Cham, took to drawing comic strips as therapy and as a way to procrastinate. Despite not having any professional training in art, Jorge mastered the craft while procrastinating and created a website (www.phdcomics.com) which now attracts many millions of visitors a year. The website's popularity is certainly a testament to how many mature students identify with the pain of colossal academic work.

In short, when faced with large assignments it is easy to feel overwhelmed by it all. So much so, that we will go to great lengths to do anything else, so long as it is marginally simpler than the task at hand.

In an interview with Nick Holzherr, a 2012 finalist from the BBC TV show *The Apprentice*, I learnt that even the most motivated people struggle in this area. However, there are a number of ways around it.

Here is what Nick had to say when I asked him about his experience of procrastination:

> 'I'll do almost everything else, including cleaning and things that I actually don't enjoy doing, just to try and not do the big task I want to do. To overcome that, I use a list and organise it by what's most important; not what's easiest or the most enjoyable. I then force myself to do the most important thing first.'

♀ Too big to start: Thinking Point & Suggestions

- **The bigger and more intimidating a task is, the more likely you are to put it off. Apart from using lists, can you think of any other ways of making your work less intimidating?**

- **Suggested reading: Chapter 9 – Goals and Planning.**

Strange assignment requirements

University is a place where the mind is supposed to be put to work. A lot of thought must be put into your assignments, otherwise your graduation certificate won't be worth much. It is no wonder, then, that lecturers have a knack of setting assignments that can have very open-ended, and at times strange, requirements. Here are some typical questions designed to stir the mind.

Philosophy – Is it better to be a human being dissatisfied than a pig satisfied; to be a Socrates dissatisfied than a fool satisfied? Discuss. (Mill, 2007)

Engineering – How would one go about building an elevator to the moon?

Sociology – What does Psy's hugely popular song, 'Gangnam Style', tell us about today's society?

Business Management – Peter Drucker once wrote, 'Management is doing *things* right; leadership is doing the *right* things.' Discuss.

We can't really fault the lecturers for setting questions like these. They make us think harder and a variety of answers can be expected. Not only that, but lecturers also hope that by broadening the scope of assignments, different students can bring different perspectives and skills to the table. In theory, these questions are more interesting than closed-ended questions, but the reality is, with such breadth and choice regarding how one can tackle the requirements also comes a certain level of decision paralysis.

While most of us think that having more choice in life is better, choice can also work against us. For instance, being presented with dozens of chocolate types makes us less likely to buy one than when presented with a handful of choices.

Likewise, having lots of different essay questions to choose from makes us less likely to pick a question that can be answered really well, when compared to having a couple questions to choose from.

The above observations come from research that showed the following:

1 Consumers are much more likely to purchase something when presented with a limited choice of varieties.
2 In the case of students (and perhaps more relevant for us), they are more likely to pick a question to answer when the question choice is more limited, and they tend to perform better on the assignments in such instances (Iyengar and Lepper, 2000).

On balance, one could say that when plenty of options exist, choice 'no longer liberates, but debilitates' (Schwartz, 2009). Thus, when presented with open-ended and broad, 'strange' assignments, beware of the propensity to be paralysed with choice. Procrastination is certainly more likely when the possibilities for how you can complete an assignment are endless than when they are limited.

Snapshot Conclusion

🕗 First, academic work that is vague is harder to start than work that seems to have detailed steps of execution. In other words, the more abstract the task, the more likely we are to procrastinate about it.

🕗 Second, when we are engaged in more enjoyable activities, the prospect of opening a book to study seems way more painful than it would be if we were to start it. Therefore, we end up procrastinating more than reality warrants.

🕗 Third, if we do not have a clue about how to start a task, it can appear to be overwhelming, and the knee-jerk reaction is to then avoid starting the work altogether.

Prevention of Pain: P-3 Diagnosis Corner

Are you procrastinating for any of the following reasons?

🕗 **Overwhelmed by the work** – Do you have an assignment that is vague and hard to understand? Does it appear too big to start?
  · See Chapter 5 and Chapter 9 for remedies.

🕗 **A preference for something more fun** – Are you lacking in motivation to start work that currently appears unappealing?
  · See Chapter 6 for remedies.

🕗 **Lacking the skills necessary for successful completion** – Does the work seem to be beyond your abilities?
  · See Chapter 6 and Chapter 9 for remedies.

4

Postponement of Punishment (or Payoff)

The Procrastination Connection

We sometimes find it easy to have fun at the expense of tomorrow precisely because the negative consequences of doing so are often delayed. Likewise, working hard today is difficult because the payoff for doing so is rarely immediate. This chapter will discuss this phenomenon and show how it is linked to putting things off.

Fun today, tragedy tomorrow

If a hangover was immediate from the moment we had an alcoholic drink, we would no doubt drink a lot less. Similarly, if we were rewarded instantaneously in our efforts to study we would no doubt be more motivated to do the work now (as opposed to later), and would indeed give in to fewer disruptive temptations. These hypothetical examples highlight some of the effects time seems to have on the way we make decisions. But we also know that there are other dimensions to choice.

Generally speaking, the decisions we make about how to behave in the moment differ not just because of the timing of consequences (as above) but also because of the size of the final outcome, or the likelihood of whatever it is that may follow on from our actions.

In effect, choice could be said to have three dimensions:

- size of consequences;
- probability of consequences; and
- timing of consequences (Green and Myerson, 2004).

So far, we have touched on how the choice to procrastinate can be related to the probability and value of payoff (Chapter 1). We have also considered how the perceived pain of starting our work and the pursuit of pleasure can thwart our efforts (Chapters 2 and 3).

However, we have yet to explore in detail how the third dimension of choice, time, influences our decisions about procrastination – more precisely, the notion that we tend to overvalue rewards now and undervalue punishments (or payoffs) in the future.

This ingredient is the fourth and final P of procrastination. I refer to it as *postponement of punishment (or payoff)*. A more poetic way of expressing the fourth P is that it refers to the tendency to undervalue the tragedy tomorrow that results from the overvalued comedy tonight.

You will note that there are two sides to the coin at play: the timing of costs and the timing of benefits (Ainslie, 2010). Both of these notions are underpinned by a bit of economic theory, so the following sections will use a few technical terms – but worry not, there is nothing new here that you haven't experienced in life already.

Hyperbolic discounting

Do you enjoy your alarm clock going off in the morning? Unless you are excited about catching a morning flight to a lavish holiday, I doubt anyone enjoys the persistent buzz of a blaring alarm. Most of us hit the snooze button for a few extra minutes of sleep, which usually then amounts to a few more minutes in bed, up until the point where the purpose of setting an early alarm is defeated altogether.

Indeed, we may have procrastinated about going to bed on time, hence the struggle to get up in the first place. But despite the late night, we decide to be wise and set a future goal of getting up early with the help of an alarm clock. However, when the requirement to wake up finally arrives, we often reject it in favour of more time in bed, despite our earlier best intentions.

In one sense, we underestimated how badly we would feel with less sleep, so we watched a bit more TV and stayed up later (i.e., postponement of punishment effects). In another sense, the next-day benefit of having enough sleep (postponement of payoff effects) was not as important as watching reruns of *Scrubs* at 11 o'clock at night (immediate rewards effects).

The result? An inability to lift heavy eyes, which forces us to hit the snooze button repeatedly in order to disarm the multiple alarms set the night before. Our immediate preference for the extra cosiness of a warm bed ends up undermining our long-run plan of waking up on time (Angeletos et al., 2001).

The above scenario is illustrative of a phenomenon which economists and psychologists call 'hyperbolic discounting' – a descriptive model and function of how human beings (and other animals) tend to behave when faced with decisions about the present and the future.

Technicalities aside, hyperbolic discounting simply means that when a choice is to be made regarding a course of action that is far away in the future, we commit to the more rational and optimal route, which may demand more patience and effort but also deliver a greater payoff later.

However, as time passes and a choice becomes imminent, we are more likely to commit to the less virtuous choice, which may require less patience and provide a smaller reward now, but also greater punishment, and/or, the loss of a larger payoff in the future (Steel, 2007). This diagram shows hyperbolic discounting in action:

Today
'I want a good grade in the future so I will start studying hard next month.'

Next month arrives
'It has now been a month but I still don't feel like studying. I will chill out for a bit longer.'

Future result
'Where did all the time go!'

💡 **Hyperbolic discounting: Thinking Point & Suggestions**

• It is easy to procrastinate and say, 'I will feel more like it tomorrow', because we undervalue the consequences of delaying our work. However, a bit of foresight and planning can help you counter this. Can you think of some ways to be more self-aware in this sense?

• Suggested reading: Chapter 9 – Goals and Planning.

Where do the above concepts fit in with procrastination? Well, if you are as confused by all this as I was, the following scenarios will help clarify and link the concepts better.

Delayed punishment

When academic punishment is imminent (e.g., missing a deadline or failing an exam), all of a sudden we become very motivated to do everything we can to meet the deadline. Last-minute cramming and pulling all-nighters are a typical response to the impeding doom, the impact of which builds up cumulatively during bouts of procrastination.

However, when punishment is postponed into the future we usually find ourselves unable to resist urges that are better off delayed until the completion of our work. In essence, the temptation to play now, instead of working, is especially amplified by the delay in consequences of putting things off (which are undervalued, given their distance in the future).

Hyperbolic discounting describes the above phenomenon further in the following way. The work–play choice becomes more challenging in the sense that only when you sit down to try and do your work do you then heavily discount the value you would get from doing something fun shortly thereafter.

For example, watching a funny YouTube video is anticipated to be more enjoyable now, as you try to do your work, rather than an hour or so later, when you may be free to watch more videos. This brings us to the next scenario.

Delayed rewards

Consider the following example, adapted from experiments a professor of psychology, Dr Stuart Vyse, often gives his students. When offered £100 or £120, it's a no-brainer to choose £120. Students only have to base their decision on the size of the reward and therefore go for the largest amount.

But how about when they are offered £100 now or £120 next month? In this scenario, more students choose the immediate £100 than wait for the distant £120. To them, £100 is worth more today than the £120 next month. However, there are cases where this preference changes.

When students are asked if they would rather receive £100 in one year, or £120 in one year plus a month, more of them opt for the £120 (Vyse, 2008). All of a sudden, students prefer to be more patient. They would rather wait one more month for the extra £20, so long as that wait happens to be a year from now (Redden, 2007). Hyperbolic discounting helps explain this change in preferences:

£100 today vs. £120 in one month	£100 in 12 months vs. £120 in 13 months
Most students will choose £100	Most students choose £120

When choices are viewed from a long-range perspective, we find it easier to commit to the wiser and more optimal route (second column in the above table). However, when the time horizon is shorter, we tend to overvalue immediate rewards (i.e., opting for the £100 now, instead of the delayed £120).

Hyperbolic discounting continued: Thinking Point & Suggestions

• It is easy to make great plans for how we are going to tackle our work. But beware: when the time comes to do it you will need all sorts of motivation and willpower to fight the effects of hyperbolic discounting.

• Suggested reading: Chapter 6 – Motivation / Chapter 7 – Willpower / Chapter 9 – Goals and Planning.

The fourth P

In sum, the fourth P of procrastination (referred to as P-4) concerns the effects of time on our behaviour. In particular, the delay of punishment for procrastination means we undervalue its impact and are therefore more likely to also postpone our work.

Furthermore, despite the ease of committing to long-term plans for working hard, when the time to knuckle down arrives, we overvalue immediate gratification and, to our ultimate disadvantage, opt not to delay small, tempting rewards.

As behavioural researchers Siegfried Dewitte and Henri Schouwenburg (2002) observed, 'procrastinators seem to suffer from strong temptations in the present, and not from weak incentives in the future'. To this I would add that procrastinators also suffer severely from the delayed consequences of procrastination. Let us now turn to considerations of how P-4 manifests itself in procrastination behaviour at university.

Manifestations of P-4

Working well under pressure

One of the most common excuses students use for procrastination is that they work better under pressure. Because the negative consequences of procrastinating are not experienced up until the night before a deadline (or after the work is submitted and a poor grade is returned), it is very easy to proclaim that pressure helps produce better work in a shorter period of time. But what happens when you actually track students' thoughts on a piece of work as the deadline creeps up on them?

Dr Pychyl carried out such a study and found that if students have a Friday deadline, on Monday they rationalise their procrastination by saying things like, 'I work better under pressure.' Yet later on in the week, say on Thursday, the very same students rarely say they are glad they delayed the work assigned them, as that gave them more pressure (Pychyl, 2008).

Sophia Barnes, a fourth-year medical student at the University of Birmingham who has a life that is busier than most students (she is mother to a 3-year-old, runs a university society, captains a judo club and still maintains high grades), told me the following when I asked her about dealing with pressure:

> 'Yes, I enjoy working under pressure. It motivates me to work and I come up with good ideas when I'm under pressure. But while some pressure is good, I don't think anyone truly comes up with their best work under lots of pressure. This is because you become so focused on getting the work done that you don't get to think around the question and explore other approaches to the problem to give a more rounded answer.'

But when I probed Sophia about how she motivated herself to start her work she responded:

> 'I try to remember how amazing it felt the first time I handed a piece of work in early, or how I felt when I aced an exam. For some reason,

remembering how horrific and stressful it feels to be rushing around, pulling all nighters, and handing things in at the last minute doesn't work for me.'

So yes, there are times when some students can manage the pressure, but in most cases it is harmful. In fact, students often report regret because they know that, given additional time, they could have done a much better job. This is in contrast to popular belief that pressure and stress frequently lead to an enhanced performance. It certainly isn't always the case and far too many examples highlight this.

In sports, for instance, we often hear of professional athletes 'choking' when under pressure; that is, performing worse despite having a high level of motivation to successfully complete a task (Dohmen, 2008). A great example of this can be seen in a study by Geir Jordet and Esther Hartman (2008).

In the study, football players who took pivotal penalties (i.e., a penalty which could lead to the loss of a match if missed) scored 30 per cent fewer goals than in less high-stake penalties where scoring a goal didn't matter as much. Jordet and Hartman hypothesised that one of the causes of a poorer performance was that the footballers were rushing through the penalty (to get it over with as soon as possible) and not preparing sufficiently.

In general, working under pressure is not the best way to go about your academic work. Procrastinators who are rushed by an impeding deadline do worse and produce more errors when compared to non-procrastinators (Ferrari, 2011).

Thinking you have plenty of time, and that you can afford to delay your work because the added pressure will help you perform better, is a dangerous

Working well under pressure: Thinking Point & Suggestions

• Are you waiting for the deadline to edge closer so that you are pumped and more motivated to work? As appealing as it may sound, this is a dangerous strategy that makes your life unnecessarily stressful.

• Suggested reading: Chapter 9 – Goals and Planning.

myth to embrace. Sure, there can be a bit of adrenaline to inspire, but sometimes this arousal leads to people confusing anxiety for excitement (Ferrari, 2011).

Planning fallacy

We are bad at planning. The iconic Sydney Opera House in Australia was supposed to be completed within roughly six years, at a cost of just $7 million. It ended up taking 15 years to complete at a hefty cost of $102 million (Hall, 1980, as cited in Buehler, Griffin and Ross, 1994).

The Millennium Dome in London (now known as the O2 Arena) is another example of overconfident planning leading to unexpected disaster. Originally budgeted to cost £500 million, it ended up costing over £1 billion (Myddelton, 2007).

Countless grandiose business projects are completed late and many end up incurring significant budget overruns. But the phenomenon is not limited to the world of business. The same planning failures that we see in large-scale capital projects also happen – albeit at a smaller scale – in our personal lives.

The mistakes business managers and government ministers make when planning how long a project will take, and how much it will cost, are indeed also made by students on a daily basis.

We grossly underestimate how long an essay will take to finish, how many hours of revision will be required to prepare for an exam, and how dire last-minute efforts can be. As a result, we procrastinate even more, on the assumption that we have plenty of time to do our work.

As optimistic tendencies when planning are so rampant, it comes as no surprise that psychologists have coined a term for the phenomenon. It is known as the *planning fallacy* – the underestimation of the time required to complete a project, despite prior insightful experiences that indicate a necessity for more time (Kahneman and Tversky, 1979).

The reason why we often succumb to the maladies of the planning fallacy is the result of a number of factors that are worth a brief mention.

First, we are generally overconfident in our talents; so much so that in a gigantic survey of one million students, it was revealed that 70 per cent rated themselves as above average in leadership ability, while a mere 2 per cent rated themselves below average (Lovallo and Kahneman, 2003). This, of course, is highly improbable. Yet numerous other studies report similar findings, such as students overestimating their performance on exams and people overestimating how quickly they can complete their work (Moore and Healy, 2007).

Second, when we have a positive outcome, for example getting a good grade despite last-minute cramming, we happily take all the credit. In contrast, if the last-minute efforts lead to failure, we more often than not play the blame game and credit our failure to external factors, such as being disrupted by friends or having other commitments.

Finally, we rarely envisage uncontrollable events disrupting our work and so do not factor in sufficient buffer time for when we may fall behind schedule. Examples of this include going to the library only to find that all copies of a required text have already been lent; or having your laptop crash and being left without a computer.

All in all, the planning fallacy is a common pitfall for many of us. While being overconfident and highly optimistic about our ability to complete a piece of work can be motivational, it also provides a false sense of comfort. Such comfort is certain to lessen the perceived impact of giving in to small temptations now, which could lead to greater punishment later.

> ## 💡 Planning fallacy: Thinking Point & Suggestions
>
> • While some students delay their work on purpose (to use the pressure for motivation), some delay their work because they overestimate how much time is left in which to do it. Has this happened to you before? Again, it is important to be self-aware in this respect in order to counter the planning fallacy.
>
> • Suggested reading: Chapter 9 – Goals and Planning.

One More Time

There are certain things in life whose impact is only manifested when the parts are taken in sum, collectively, and cumulatively, across a very long period of time. Smoking is one example. Having one more cigarette is not the difference between getting cancer or not. Another example is the environment: one more car on the road is not the difference between global warming or a lack thereof (MacIntosh, 2010).

Likewise in student life: watching one more cat video on YouTube is not the difference between passing and failing an exam. One more tweet, status update or phone call to a friend is rarely ever pivotal in deciding how successful you will be in completing the work you are assigned. And because we know this, we do not give much thought to the delayed consequences that are due to arise when these small failings in willpower cumulatively add up to disastrous results.

Unfortunately, it is rare to have a clear turning point where we can see that the extra cigarette will cause cancer, the extra car will increase global warming, or that the additional YouTube clip of a brave goat attacking pedestrians will lead to us failing to meet our deadlines. Indeed, this is partly what makes such small-scale day-to-day decisions so difficult. As behavioural economists Ted O'Donoghue and Matthew Rabin (2000) put it, this is the area 'where self-control problems are most likely to influence behaviour'.

In any event, spending just a bit more time procrastinating seems harmless when taken in isolation. And, as previously mentioned, it is hard to determine when one additional stint of procrastination will seal our fate. For these reasons we end up indulging in temptations more than we really should, all the while ignoring the cumulative impact they have on our long-term plans and goals. Such a micro perspective (as opposed to macro), can only serve to increase procrastination behaviours.

♀ One more time: Thinking Point & Suggestions

• Are there little things you do a lot of that have added up to adverse consequences? Checking your social networks frequently, for example? Whatever these things are, try reflecting on their cumulative impact and you may find it easier to reason against over-indulging in them.

• Suggested reading: Chapter 7 – Willpower / Chapter 8 – Focus and Attention.

Snapshot Conclusion

↻ First, procrastination has no immediate repercussions. Since consequences are delayed and far off in the future, we continue to put off our work until we fully appreciate the urgency of a looming deadline.

↻ Second, despite making long-term plans to work hard, when the time finally arrives to do so, immediate and small temptations are preferred over delayed larger payoffs.

↻ Third, overconfidence in our abilities often leads us to underestimate how long a task will take. We then erroneously take comfort in the belief that we have more time than there really is.

↻ Fourth, given the fact that one stint of procrastination is rarely pivotal to the successful completion of a task, and that we do not know where that pivot point is, we end up delaying our work and indulging in little bits of fun more than we should.

Postponement of Punishment (or Payoff): P-4 Diagnosis Corner

Are you procrastinating for any of the following reasons?

↻ **No harm done** – Do you lack an appreciation of the future consequences of having a bit more fun now?
  · See Chapter 6 for remedies, in particular, the section on how to give long-term aims a piggyback.

↻ **Strong temptations** – While working, do you get the urge to check out every little notification that pops up on your phone?
  · See Chapter 7 and Chapter 8 for remedies.

↻ **Overconfidence** – Do you prefer working under pressure? Or do you often fail to plan sufficient time to complete your work?
  · See Chapter 9 for advice, especially the section on planning.

Part 2

How to Beat Procrastination

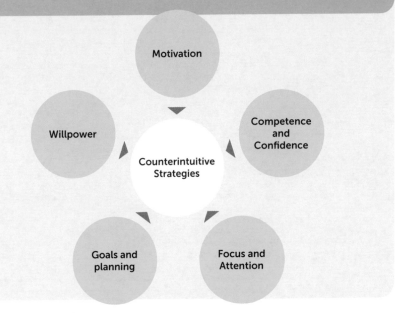

To minimise procrastination you must arm yourself with a range of strategies to combat it in all of its unique forms. This part of the book will provide guidance on fundamental areas (Competence and Confidence, Motivation, Willpower, Focus and Attention, Goals and Planning) that are vital to defeating the habit. Alternative strategies that draw from these fundamentals will also be suggested, in the final chapter on counterintuitive strategies.

5

Competence and Confidence

The Procrastination Connection

Having the skills required to successfully complete a task and the belief that you can do so can be a powerful way of alleviating the maladies of the first P of procrastination. This chapter will offer insights on how to increase your competence, self-efficacy and confidence. In doing so, you will be able to better deal with procrastination that stems from not being sure about yourself.

Skills and beliefs

In Chapter 1, we learnt that self-efficacy is how much confidence we have in our ability to successfully complete an assignment. If we lack in self-efficacy, we are likely to avoid doing challenging academic work that may be assigned to us. Indeed, if something is hard and we don't believe in our capabilities to do it, we usually procrastinate about it.

Moreover, a healthy amount of self-efficacy can be advantageous and there is now a large body of research that shows that self-efficacy contributes to student motivation, achievement and learning (Van Dinther, Dochy and Segers, 2011). In fact, self-efficacy has been shown to be a reliable predictor of academic performance (Lane et al., 2003).

Students with healthy levels of self-efficacy are more persistent, hard working, and are more likely to take on more difficult courses (Linnenbrink and Pintrich, 2002). That said, too much self-efficacy or overconfidence – as we learnt in Chapter 4 – can be disastrous. If students falsely believe that they can finish an essay or pass an exam with one night's worth of effort, they are merely setting themselves up for calamity.

The key, therefore, is to have a realistic but somewhat optimistic amount of self-efficacy (Linnenbrink and Pintrich, 2002). How can we enhance such an attribute in order to battle procrastination? Here are some tips based on social cognitive theory and the work of the prominent psychologist Albert Bandura (1977).

Develop mastery

The most powerful and authentic way you can build self-efficacy is by having personal evidence of past accomplishments at the specific task at hand (or something similar). When people successfully overcome difficult challenges, they become more confident in their ability to overcome similar challenges in the future.

Moreover, education and sports psychologists advise that self-efficacy is further enhanced if someone is successful at a task with the following characteristics:

- it is especially tough;
- little external assistance is provided; and
- there are clear signs of progress (Feltz, Short and Sullivan, 2008).

This is in contrast to tasks that are completed easily, with lots of help from other people. These tasks do not build a robust sense of self-efficacy (Van Dinther, Dochy and Segers, 2011).

In addition to the above, repeated failures can eat away at self-efficacy and so you can't just fake it till you make it. Your mind needs reliable data before it can generate confidence.

Therefore, if you find yourself procrastinating because you are unsure of your ability to do well, try and reflect on past examples where you were faced with a similar challenging assignment but went on to successfully complete it.

Alternatively, if you cannot think of examples of past success, start creating them in your life. Take on challenging work or try learning a new skill. It is possible for success in one area to breed confidence in another, especially if you take credit for your hard work and don't just attribute it to pure luck (Pintrich and Schunk, 2002, cited by Margolis, 2005).

A good example of this is how people deal with phobias. It isn't unusual, for example, for people who overcome a phobia specific to one animal to find it easier to overcome phobias with other animals, as well as phobias in social contexts (Bandura, 1977).

Another way of enhancing self-efficacy is by simply breaking a difficult task down into little pieces. By successfully completing each miniature block of what may be a demanding assignment, you will gain increased confidence in completing the larger whole. Psychologists sometimes refer to such mini-tasks as proximal goals, which are known to enhance skill development and self-efficacy more effectively than big, distant goals (Zimmerman, 2000) (more on this in Chapter 9).

Generally speaking, self-efficacy draws from past experiences. Setting yourself a gruelling challenge and taking on the risk of looking silly as a beginner may not be the easiest path to success, but it is the surest path to a robust sense of self-efficacy.

So try learning a new language, dance, sport, musical instrument, or whatever takes your fancy. Having a wide array of multiple, worthwhile successes in life will mean that whenever something challenging comes up, you are better able to infer from past experiences the confidence in your ability to adapt and persist in difficult times.

> **Practical Application**
>
> If you have exams coming up and are procrastinating about revision, try using past exam questions as a basis for your studies. They provide excellent mastery experiences because if you can progressively do well in a mock, you will feel more confident about your revision efforts and will be less likely to put off revising.

Seek inspiration

Another way of building self-efficacy is to seek inspiration from people who have successfully completed a task before. Psychologists argue that this is particularly effective when we find examples of people who are similar to us and are therefore easier to relate to (Margolis, 2005). The notion, 'if he or she can do it, so can I', can be a good way of convincing ourselves that we have a decent chance of doing well at something.

Therefore, look to friends who have overcome difficult challenges. Read an inspiring autobiography or two. If you have siblings at university, ask them how they are getting on, or even consider chatting to recent graduates who successfully managed the demands of university.

I certainly learnt a lot from, and was inspired by, the students I interviewed for this book. We all struggle with procrastination and no one is perfectly immune from the habit, so it can be particularly helpful chatting to friends to see how they deal with it.

In sum, if you are struggling with revision or coursework, chatting to a friend who has passed the exam in question or successfully completed similar coursework could provide inspiration and a renewed sense of self-efficacy on your part.

Practical Application

Are you nervous about an upcoming class presentation? Are you needlessly delaying to prepare for it? Find students who are good at public speaking and ask them if they ever feel nervous before going on stage. You will learn that they, too, get nerves, but go on to do well because of sufficient practice and preparation. Be sure to also ask these students for any tips and advice on how to do better.

Get early feedback

It is entirely possible for someone to be verbally persuaded and convinced by other people that they possess the capability of mastering a difficult situation (Bandura, 1977). In other words, words of encouragement can go a long way in building your self-efficacy, but only if they are genuine and come from a credible source (Bong and Skaalvik, 2003).

Therefore, as you work your way through early drafts, consider discussing your progress with the people who have assigned the work to you. Getting feedback in the early stages has been shown to spur procrastinators on to complete their work earlier than usual. This is probably the result of constructive and motivational feedback, the process of discussing the work, or the creation of earlier self-imposed deadlines (Fritzsche, Rapp Young and Hickson, 2003).

So long as you seek feedback from people you consider to be knowledgeable and reliable, you may find yourself receiving a boost in your confidence to be successful in the work you are assigned. But note, psychologists advise that self-efficacy is only enhanced if the feedback is positive and constructive.

Too much negative feedback, on the other hand, can be detrimental. Here is what one student at Nottingham Trent University shared with me when I interviewed him:

'I recently completed a CELTA (Certificate in Teaching English to Speakers of Other Languages) as an addition to my degree. It started off well but the constant criticism has now finally given me a fear of failure to the point that I don't feel confident about teaching. This is ironic, as before my final year I had taught people English and felt confident. This is something I now no longer have.'

With the above in mind, try to place more emphasis on feedback that encourages you by tying your current efforts to past successes. This is more effective than critique that reminds you of your failures.

Furthermore, pay particular attention to appraisal that provides immediate error corrections, as this is more effective than feedback that ignores mistakes in your work (Margolis, 2005).

> **Practical Application**
>
> Dissertations have great feedback mechanisms because each student is assigned a supervisor who provides feedback and discussion sessions during the writing process. In other assignments, there might not be any formal support; however, all lecturers have office hours during which you can visit and ask questions about your course material.
>
> Try to arrange an appointment with your lecturer and use this as an opportunity to discuss progress on your assignments. Indeed, merely having an appointment with your lecturer could spur you on to complete a section of your work sooner in order to be able to discuss it.

Watch your emotional state

Emotions can be powerful in determining how confident we feel. For example, imagine having to go to a salsa class as a complete beginner. The utterly confusing, body-twisting beso – a move beginners should hold off attempting until they've learnt the basics – would either look like good fun if you were cheerful, or a complete nightmare if you were overly stressed, tense and anxious.

You see, experiencing negative emotions as we approach a task can sometimes be interpreted as a signal of forthcoming failures, and this has the ability to weaken our sense of self-efficacy. But such tensions aren't always bad. If you already have a robust sense of self-efficacy, tension can be energising. If, on the other hand, you already doubt your abilities, you may interpret such tension as a sign of weakness (Van Dinther, Dochy and Segers, 2011).

While emotions don't necessarily have the strongest influence on self-efficacy (in fact, some psychologists argue they have the weakest impact), they are still worth thinking about as there is a risk that they may amplify feelings of incompetence (Margolis, 2005). Not only that, such feelings (as we saw in Chapter 2) can at times lead to more impulsive behaviour. So, as well as aiming for mastery, seeking inspiration and getting early feedback, try to always be mindful about your feelings.

Practical Application

Students often complain about a lack of energy, not feeling like it, or not being in the mood to face challenging academic work. If you are feeling like this, try taking on the less strenuous parts of your work. That way, some progress can still be made. Alternatively, try combining something fun with your work. Guidance on how to do this is provided in the following chapter on Motivation (pp. 72–3).

Perfectionism and fear of failure

Perfectionism and fear of failure are often touted as a common cause of procrastination but, as we saw in Chapter 1, they do not always contribute greatly to procrastination. Indeed, there is a harmful and a positive side to being a perfectionist. Likewise, a fear of failure can be both damaging or energising. That said, if you struggle with either perfectionism or a fear of failure, the following tips may help.

Do first, improve later

Throw out external expectations and start working now! Don't worry too much about the quality of your work in the early stages. As long as you start something, you can always improve it later. After all, it is better to have a rubbish draft to mould than no work at all.

Brittany Binowski, a New York University graduate who has worked at Forbes and written for the *Huffington Post*, had this to say:

'I think, for me, when it gets to that point, especially in writing, when I'm worried about it being perfect, it's just one of those things where I have to get something down. I don't care if it's right or anything. I go from there and see what comes out.

And then after I do that, I just keep going back and working with it, and shaping it from there. I think that's the hardest thing, getting stuff on paper. Once you do that, then everything becomes a little easier.'

But if perfection is not sought, what would success look like? When I spoke to Brittany more about the topic, she reiterated what matters more: 'knowing I'm trying my hardest and getting better'.

So don't worry too much about the 'details' in the early stages. Starting can be tough if you are concerned with producing the very best work immediately, but not if you are OK with a 'rough' draft.

> ### Practical Application
>
> **Finding it hard to start an essay? Forget the introduction. Forget the conclusion. Forget all structure and just try writing one paragraph that makes one simple point. Sometimes you won't know what to write until you actually start writing.**

After making a start, you will find that you gain momentum and things get slightly easier. So forget perfect, for it is usually just an excuse for not getting started. Instead, be okay with starting rough, and then focus on doing your very best to improve at a later stage.

Focus on you, not others

A large amount of procrastination goes on unnoticed in lecture halls and classrooms. The majority of students are guilty of it (including me) and I am certain you have succumbed to it at some point as well. Let me explain.

Have you ever found yourself not raising your hand to ask a question during a lecture out of a fear of looking stupid? That, my friend, is a classic example of procrastination that is driven by a fear of failure, perfectionist tendencies, and worrying too much about what other people think.

When we base our self-worth on reputation alone, it holds us back from taking on challenging tasks and frequently contributes to feelings of anxiety, depression and low self-esteem (Neumeister, 2004). To prevent this, when approaching a piece of work, try not to be overly concerned with what people will think of it.

While official assessments, feedback and criticisms should not be ignored, allowing them to define you and taking them personally is not healthy. Instead, be forward-looking and focus on personal improvement and mastery. One way of achieving this is to benchmark your current work against work you have done in the past and aiming to do better in a specific area of weakness.

> **Practical Application**
>
> **If you receive a poor mark on an assignment and all you do is compare yourself to higher performing peers, you may find yourself demotivated. A better approach is to get feedback on your weak areas (e.g., academic referencing, structure, logic of arguments) and work to get better at them.**

Perfect is impossible but excellence is applaudable

Michael J. Fox, the Canadian actor who rose to fame with the blockbuster movie franchise *Back to the Future*, once said:

> 'I am careful not to confuse excellence with perfection. Excellence I can reach for, perfection is God's business.'

In other words, perfect is impossible. Given limited time and energy, there is only so much you can do. Indeed, you have to be careful not to set unrealistic standards whereby you meticulously work away at perfecting bits of your work, all the while ignoring the need for balance. I learnt this lesson quickly while preparing for a chartered accountancy qualification exam.

In the final four-hour case study paper, if you answered one or two of the three requirements perfectly but provided an incomplete answer to just one requirement, you would most certainly fail. Students who spent too long on one part of the exam, trying to perfect their answers, ended up missing out on generally easier marks in other areas.

The same can be said of all other assignments we are tasked with academically. You have a limited amount of time and the best you can ever do will rarely ever be perfect. It can, however, be excellent – that is, extremely good, with sufficient coverage of key areas.

Therefore, as long as you can identify the main themes or aspects of your work and cover them well, you can excel without the need for being perfect. Dr Gordon Flett, a leading researcher on the topic of perfectionism and the role it plays in psychopathology, sums it up best:

> Students should work strenuously – but not obsessively – in order to achieve their goals. The goals should focus on excellence and doing well rather than being flawless. (York U, 2012)

Practical Application

Procrastination can sometimes mask itself when we spend far too long planning, researching or revising any one topic. If you notice this in your efforts, take a step back and look at the larger picture. Ask yourself whether it is really worth going into such a level of detail and perfection in any one area.

Snapshot Conclusion

- First, students who have a healthy level of self-efficacy are more persistent and hard working. Such students also procrastinate less than students who have low levels of self-efficacy.
- Second, having more mastery experiences, seeking inspiration and having regular feedback can contribute to increased self-efficacy. Provided these factors are in place, procrastination can be reduced significantly.
- Third, perfectionism and fear of failure tendencies can be reduced if we are less concerned with rough drafts and what other people think of our efforts, and if we don't get too drawn into trying to reach unrealistic and impossible goals. This, too, should help you minimise procrastination.

6

Motivation

The Procrastination Connection

Motivation is a self-evident solution to reducing procrastination. But what exactly drives us to do our work? This chapter will briefly explore key motivation theories and provide pragmatic steps you can to take to harness the power of your interests, drive and incentives.

Intrinsic and extrinsic motivation

Flick through students' status updates on social networking sites during an exam period and the topic of motivation (or lack thereof) is not uncommon. When faced with upcoming exams or coursework deadlines, we moan about being bored with the work, not having the energy to start or not seeing the relevance of the effort required. Such musings are just a few of the motivational precursors that emerge prior to procrastination.

But as we all know, motivation is a pivotal ingredient in getting things done. Motivation is what *moves* us to do something (Ryan and Deci, 2000a). Without the drive to start or persist in our work, procrastination is inevitable; particularly when that lack of drive to engage with your work is used as an excuse to pursue other, irrelevant activities.

Fortunately, there are many ways of motivating yourself; so much so that the topic is perhaps best served with a book of its own. Regardless, I will share with you a portion of the highlights in the area – that is, a strategy that deals with our levels of interest and engagement, a strategy that deals with the concept of utility, as well as an idea that deals with our impulsive nature.

Cultivate intrinsic interests

For superior motivation, you should always try to find something intrinsically interesting about the work that you are doing. Decades of research show that being intrinsically motivated – driven to do something because it is genuinely interesting, enjoyable or because it contributes to self-development – is a more powerful form of motivation than doing something for the sake of extrinsic outcomes such as money, status, or even grades (Ryan and Deci, 2000a).

Consider how you feel when you are doing something you naturally enjoy, a hobby perhaps. In such cases, how often do you complain about feeling tired when it comes to engaging in the activity? How often do you complain about boredom? In fact, how often do you procrastinate in hobby-related matters?

My guess is that you rarely ever find yourself delaying things for which you have a passion. As it is, people who are intrinsically motivated procrastinate less (Lee, 2005) and also tend to outperform those with purely extrinsic motivations.

Let me share with you an experiment that highlights this idea in a university context. In a study by Vansteenkiste and colleagues (2004), marketing students were tasked with reading a piece of text on business communication styles.

Half the students were told that carefully reading the assigned text would contribute to their personal growth (the intrinsic-goal condition), while the other half were told that it would help them land a well-paying job (the extrinsic-goal condition).

At the end of the study the students' understanding of the material was tested as follows: they participated in a small group presentation where they were graded, and also had to complete a written test. To no surprise, students in the intrinsic-goal condition outperformed those in the extrinsic-goal condition. They enjoyed the learning process more, got higher grades, and demonstrated higher persistence in the task.

In light of the above, an obvious strategy with regard to higher motivation is to first try and choose only those things for which you are intrinsically motivated; things that have some personal meaning to you and for which you have a genuine interest in. (You may have already done so by choosing a university course that seemed appealing.)

However, since we do not always have the luxury of just doing the things that are inherently fun, the next alternative is to frame something uninteresting in a way that engages you intrinsically.

For example, in the experiment described earlier, students' intrinsic motivation was induced by telling them that completing a certain task would contribute to their personal growth. In a different experiment by the same researchers, intrinsic motivation was induced by telling students that doing Tai-bo led to health benefits. (On the contrary, students who were told that doing Tai-bo exercises led to physical attractiveness ended up performing worse and persisting less than those who were directed to a personal growth goal.)

In sum, if you can frame your work in an intrinsically engaging way, you will be able to tap into a superior, more robust form of motivation. This is why, for example, students who find tasks personally meaningful are often more productive than those who see no personal meaning in their work (Ariely, Kamenica and Prelec, 2008).

While it certainly takes some reflection, connecting the task at hand to a specific goal that is personally meaningful to you might just be the way to gear yourself into action (Vansteenkiste et al., 2009).

> **Practical Application**
>
> **An accounting student who has a passion for entrepreneurship but absolutely hates a certain tax module and can't find any motivation to study it could reframe their attitude by considering the following: 'How will this topic help me with my personal growth and desire to become a talented business man or woman in the future? Perhaps if I understand tax reliefs, tax rates, and corporate structures better, I will become a much better entrepreneur in the future.'**

Seek utility

The nature of university work is such that there are some things you will be genuinely interested in and some things you won't find deeply meaningful regardless of how much mind-bending you attempt. For example, a first-year mathematics student who does not find any pleasure in doing vector algebra will struggle for motivation if he or she is unable to see the point of mastering the topic and understand how it relates to anything they care about.

The alternative, then, is to consider the lesser of all other evils: that is, to seek a type of extrinsic motivation that is *of your own choosing*. It is important to note 'of your own choosing' because studies indicate that when our actions are purely regulated by external powers (for example, doing work to avoid punishment or to please parents), we end up being less energised about the task and therefore perform worse and persist less in our efforts (Ryan and Deci, 2000b).

As previously hinted at, extrinsic motivation is when you are moved to do something for external outcomes that are separable from the activity itself (Vansteenkiste, Lens and Deci, 2006). While this form of motivation is not as robust or as long-lasting as intrinsic motivation, seeking some form of utility from your work can help you to tap into a reserve tank of drive.

Can't be bothered to start an essay? Think about how starting early might help you produce better work. Then consider how a higher grade could enhance your degree classification and, ultimately, the graduate job opportunities that will be available to you.

The above is an example of what psychologists call *identified regulation*. It is when you place personal importance on a task and pursue it out of your own free will (Ryan and Deci, 2000a). Additionally, by understanding that something will be of use, you become more motivated to work at it. On the other hand, when an assignment seems to have no particular relevance or application outside of university, motivation declines.

That being said, given how abstract and theoretical university assign-ments can be, it is always worth reflecting upon how mastering a topic (in revision, for example) or getting started on an essay can contribute to your life in practical terms. As with intrinsic interest, this reflection can be difficult. So below, I conclude with a few examples I came across on how motivation can be enhanced by seeking utility in a task.

In an inspirational article titled 'Developing students' appreciation for what is taught in school', educational psychologist Dr Jere Brophy (2008) provided examples of how the value of education could be better articulated, which I summarise here:

Writing empowers you with the skill of communication with others and also allows you to preserve ideas or observations that matter to you.
Mathematics provides you with the skills to better quantify worldly matters.
Geography can be used to highlight reasons for variations in economic and social activities of nations.
History teaches you lessons that have stood the test of time and are as applicable today as they were in earlier ages.
Literature can reveal to you the components of a good story (e.g., plot, conflicts, resolutions, protagonists etc).

Practical Application

A mathematics student bored with vectors and matrix exercises could motivate themselves by reflecting on the vivid applications of the topic. For instance, while vectors are an abstract concept, the practical applications range from encryption to computer graphics (we would not have special effects today if it weren't for this area of mathematics). The student may therefore consider how this topic may be used in their future work in the computer graphics industry (if that is an industry of interest).

Give long-term aims a piggyback

In Chapter 4, we learnt that the delay of negative consequences for putting off work makes it easier to procrastinate. Furthermore, we learnt that when the rewards associated with getting our work done on time are far off, our sense of urgency is diluted. On the other hand, when the punishment or rewards associated with our efforts are more immediate, we are moved to complete our work earlier (Thakkar, 2009).

The problem of motivation therefore sometimes arises from temporal effects (i.e., the effects of time). That is, we discount future events heavily and in the short term have a tendency to seek out immediate gratification despite a future cost. This is in contrast to persevering now, in exchange for a larger, later, reward.

But there is hope. We can turn the above weakness into a strength by utilising an idea that psychologists and behavioural economists refer to as *impulse-pairing*. This is where you 'piggyback' a distant goal on one or more of your impulsive tendencies. Dr Piers Steel, in citing Ainslee (1992), provides a brilliant example of this:

> Let's say someone has a long-term goal of giving to charity but just can't motivate themselves to do it, especially as they are often lured by the act of gambling. This person can still meet their charitable motives by indulging in a casino night at a local church. This way, their long-term interest of being charitable is achieved by pairing it to a short-term impulse (gambling). (Steel, 2007)

In a university setting, the same principle can be applied in a number of ways. For instance, forming study groups can help extraverted students meet their academic demands while also meeting their need to interact with other students.

So, if you are finding it hard to engage with your work, think of ways you can piggyback it on a guilty pleasure. Here is how Benjamin O'Hare, an undergraduate at the London College of Communication, uses this technique in the context of study motivation:

'Having to listen to someone speak for a very long time with no breaks for questions or any visuals to further illustrate the topic can not only be boring, but it can destroy any motivation I had for learning the subject. As such, there have been times where finding a TED talk video [www.ted.com] on the subject has been able to not only convey the points better, but lead me to want to learn more about the topic.'

Practical Application

An English literature student who cannot find any motivation to study the Romantic era can use their love of film to get started on the subject. They may decide to watch movies set in the era (e.g., *Pride and Prejudice*, 2005) or movies based on themes of the era (e.g., *Interview With the Vampire*, 1996). In either case, scaffolding a guilty pleasure onto something academically useful can go a long way in countering procrastination.

Snapshot Conclusion

- First, students with intrinsic motivation procrastinate less (Senécal, Koestner and Vallerand, 1995), work harder, and outperform those with purely extrinsic motivation. Therefore, either choose work that you will enjoy or try to frame your assignments in a way that brings personal meaning.
- Second, if you cannot find anything inherently interesting in your work, think about its practical applications and whether it can serve you in some way, today or in the future.

꙳ Third, for an even more unique form of motivation, consider using your guilty pleasures in a manner that provides a piggyback to your long-term goals.

7

Willpower

The Procrastination Connection

You must dig deep for self-control and discipline to start your work early. Likewise, the power to say no to all manner of distractions is vital if you are to persevere in your academic efforts. This chapter provides suggestions and insights as to how you can build your willpower muscles and also offers alternatives for when such reserves are depleted.

A scarce resource

IQ scores are pretty good at predicting academic performance. But they are often outdone by other factors (as we learnt with the notion of grit in Chapter 2). Take self-discipline, self-control or willpower (words I will use interchangeably to refer to the same idea), for example. They refer to our ability to regulate behaviours, thoughts and emotions (de Ridder et al., 2012). Such competences are a far better predictor of academic achievement than IQ.

More specifically, researchers Angela Duckworth and Martin Seligman (2005) found that highly self-disciplined students spent more time on their work, had higher grades, and that they started their assignments earlier than students with less self-control.

But self-control is not just something you are born with, nor is it an endless resource we can draw from to overcome distractions and to persevere in our work. Recent developments on the topic indicate that willpower is, in fact, like a muscle. So, for example, when people are tempted with chocolate and are asked to resist eating it, their resistance to subsequent temptations weakens (Baumeister, 1998).

In other words, willpower can be fatigued. Psychologists call this ego-depletion, the effects of which have been reported in over 100 studies (Inzlicht and Schmeichel, 2012). In light of the above phenomenon – that our willpower weakens after being used – in this chapter I will share with you a number of ways to better manage willpower so as to combat procrastination.

Build willpower muscle

The notion that you can build your willpower muscles has been evidenced in numerous studies, some more interesting (or bizarre) than others. For instance, at a tech conference in 2012, a team of German psychologists and designers revealed a chocolate machine designed to help people train for increased self-control (Bennett, 2012).

The machine operates as follows: every 40 to 60 minutes it dispenses a scrumptious chocolate ball. The user of the machine can then either give in to their desire and eat the chocolate or place it back into the machine (the decision is tracked by a counter).

In a trial study involving the machine, students were told that they were free to eat the chocolate that was dispensed by the gadget. However, they were also told that if they could resist eating the chocolate it would help them train their self-control.

At the end of the experiment, the researchers found that while people initially found it hard to resist eating the chocolates, over the course of two weeks, daily efforts to resist the chocolate resulted in the students finding it easier and easier to refrain from the indulgence (Kehr et al., 2012). It turns out that the mere act of repeatedly overcoming temptation can enhance future battles with our impulsive desires.

Fortunately, researchers have not been short on creativity when it comes to training willpower muscle. In a number of other experiments, participants have been tasked with frequently expending willpower to work on their posture, brush their teeth, avoid curse words, or adhere to exercise plans.

In doing the above, the participants have been found to have increased self-control not just in these areas, but across other parts of their life as well (Hagger et al., 2010).

Moreover, in a university setting, studies also indicate that students who repeatedly practise self-control have improved study habits, are better at dealing with exam stress, and are better equipped to deal with a diverse range of temptations. Indeed these students find themselves better at resisting addictive indulgences such as alcohol, cigarettes, junk food, and even TV (Oaten and Cheng, 2006b).

One study, for instance, found that students who took up a disciplined exercise regime over the course of two months also realised self-control improvements in their academic life (Oaten and Cheng, 2006b). What this means for you and me is that in our fight against procrastination, we would do well in having our capacity for discipline trained in whatever way possible.

In sum, regularly overcoming temptation can go a long way in enhancing your ability to persist in your studies. Sure, it can be tiring to face such battles, but in the long term, like physical exercise, it makes you stronger (Oaten and Cheng, 2006b). As procrastination is sometimes a battle between how powerful impulsive urges are and how strong your willpower is, having a larger set of willpower-biceps is bound to be advantageous.

Pre-commit

The story of Odysseus, a figure from Greek mythology who is often mentioned in procrastination and self-control literature, has a surprising lesson for those of us who sometimes cannot muster enough willpower to overcome strong temptations.

> **Practical Application**
>
> A student who leads a sedentary life and finds it hard not to be interrupted by social network website notifications could benefit from taking up a disciplined exercise regime. As demonstrated in the study by Oaten and Cheng discipline in one area often spills over into other areas of life. This student might therefore benefit from building their self-discipline through exercise, which could influence their behaviour towards university work. Other ways of building such discipline include having a strict work schedule or habitualised efforts (more on this later).

In the story, Odysseus and his crew have to pass an island full of Sirens – creatures with such beautiful voices that no crew could resist the lure of their songs. Moreover, these were songs that killed men. Sailors who were attracted by the voices would blindly sail towards the island only to find death and destruction among reefs that no one other than the Sirens themselves could navigate.

What did Odysseus do to avoid such a fate? He told his men to fill their ears with wax so that they could not hear the Sirens' songs. He then asked his crew to bind him to the ship's mast. This way, he would not turn the ship towards the dangerous island if the Sirens sang their songs to lure him. Furthermore, he commanded his crew not to untie him no matter how much he pleaded.

The lesson? Committing in advance can help, particularly in moments of weak self-control. And, like Odysseus, having supportive comrades (or friends in our case) can also be advantageous.

Interestingly, willpower expert and researcher Dr Roy Baumeister advises that pre-commitment – the act of binding yourself to a virtuous path in advance – is generally safer than facing temptations head-on (Baumeister and Tierney, 2011). Baumeister provides the following example: a gambler is better off placing their name on a casino's list of people who can't collect winnings. Another example is how a dieter is better off not stocking their fridge with bacon and ice cream. And likewise, a student is better off disabling the Internet all together, if they wish to avoid the lures of YouTube, Tumblr, Facebook and so forth.

It is not uncommon for students to use all manner of pre-commitment devices to beat procrastination. Here is what Chris Rowlands, a first-year law student at the University of Cambridge, uses to bind himself to the task at hand:

> 'Self-enforcement can be pretty difficult – that ongoing battle between the productive brain and the procrastination brain can really start to wear down your defences.
>
> With that said, I have a program which blocks access to websites for a set period of time, which is really useful. As soon as you realise you can't procrastinate that way, you accept that you might as well just get on and work.'

The temptations we face when attempting to engage academic work can be extremely powerful. The Internet, mobile phones, and the social lures of student halls and accommodation present challenges that are especially unique to the student population. These are powerful forces, so do not underestimate them. Consider using pre-commitment devices to stop you from succumbing to their lure.

Practical Application

Can't stop checking your Facebook page? Something as simple as deactivating your account during academically demanding times is a simple pre-commitment device many students have used successfully. Another application of pre-commitment could be to work without a computer in a university library, as opposed to staying in your student accommodation where flatmates and friends can easily distract you from your work.

Habitualise your efforts

How much willpower do you expend in having to brush your teeth everyday? Very little, I should hope. You probably don't remember it but as a child it is likely that you protested and wrestled with your parents about having to brush your teeth before bedtime. Nonetheless, over the years the habit went onto autopilot such that, today, hardly any willpower is required to brush your teeth before going to bed.

As willpower is a limited resource, we must be thrifty in its use. In the previous sections we looked at how strengthening your willpower muscles and using pre-commitment devices can help. But these strategies are not always effective. Therefore, it is worth considering the alternative alluded to in the childhood anecdote above – the formation of good habits.

Habits can be powerful because they tend to persist, even when willpower is depleted. Take, for example, students whose willpower was depleted in an experiment where they had to use their weak hand for two days. With fatigued willpower the students were less likely to carry out non-routine activities that required self-control. On the other hand, most of their usual habits persisted. If the students had healthy habits such as going to the gym, they continued to do so. But likewise, if they had poor dietary habits (perhaps an addiction to doughnuts), those too were maintained (Neal, Wood and Quinn, 2006).

Therefore, if we are able to automate behaviours that can help us work more effectively, we reduce our reliance on willpower, which can be saved for more intense challenges if not already depleted.

Indeed, psychologists point out that good performances at school are 'rarely a matter of single, prodigious acts of willpower'. Instead, it is the students who maintain consistent and steady effort throughout the academic year who go on to perform better (de Ridder et al., 2012).

In your studies, look for ways of making your work more routine and habitualised. This may be starting and finishing your work at a specific time every day (as I did when revising for my final-year university exams) or it could involve writing a paragraph of an essay each day. Regardless of the habit, so long as it enables you to work a little on your work each day, you can avoid the procrastinator's nightmare of doing all-nighters and producing poor quality work at the very last minute.

Practical Application

A computer science student who has weekly lab assignments can benefit from making a habit of always starting them the day they are received. At first it will be hard, but after a few weeks of sustained effort it can become second nature to start working early.

Snapshot Conclusion

- First, self-control and willpower are vital in defeating procrastination, as it is such virtues that help us persist in our work. More precisely, willpower helps us not to succumb to the pursuit of task-irrelevant activities.
- Second, willpower is very much like a muscle. It can tire but it can also be strengthened with practice.
- Third, in light of the above, look for ways of strengthening your willpower muscles. This will usually involve implementing activities in your life that require frequent acts of self-discipline.
- Fourth, there will be times when your willpower runs out and therefore it is useful to have other strategies to hand. Pre-commitment devices and habitualised efforts can help in such instances.

8

Focus and Attention

The Procrastination Connection

Willpower can help fend off disruptions as you attempt to work. But there are also other measures that can serve you well. This chapter will explore strategies that involve your environment, body and mind, and engagement. In these areas you will find more ways of curbing harmful levels of procrastination.

Staying on track

There are times when we find it easy to start our work. But once we get on track, the problem changes to that of *staying* on track, and this is what this chapter is primarily concerned with.

As we saw in earlier parts of the book, disruption spirals, boredom, and work that is mentally painful are just a few examples of what makes staying on track especially difficult. It is for these reasons that we must now turn to ways of enhancing focus and attention – skills that can help you further in avoiding the lures of disruption to get through difficult academic work.

Environment

In Chapter 7, we learnt of pre-commitment devices that can protect you from tempting distractions. A way to take this further is to optimise your work environment such that it is conducive to your efforts. In order to do this, it is worth noting what science has to say on matters of attention, influential cues and subsequent response behaviours.

Consider the following experiment, carried out by researchers Traci Mann and Andrew Ward (2004). In the study, dieters were split into two groups. One group was placed in a room containing noticeable food items (food cues) while the other was placed in a room with diet books and a weighing scale (diet cues).

Once settled, the participants had to engage in either a demanding mental task (memorising a 9-digit number) or a light-weight mental task (remembering a 1-digit number); they were also provided with a delicious fatty milkshake and told they could drink as much of it as they wanted.

Group 1 (Food cues)

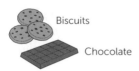

Biscuits

Chocolate

Group 2 (Diet cues)

Diet books

Weighing scales

This experiment is a personal favourite because the results are counterintuitive and reveal how powerful environments can be when the mind is at work. Read on to see what the researchers found.

Participants who were faced with a difficult mental task were highly susceptible to environment cues. That is, dieters who had to remember a 9-digit number ended up drinking almost twice as much milkshake when in a room with food items (Group 1) compared to a room with diet books and weighing scales (Group 2).

Moreover, dieters who had the easier task of remembering a one-digit number were not so easily influenced by the environment, regardless of whether the room had diet or food cues.

Similar results have been noticed with smoking. When demands are placed on attention and the mind is hard at work, smokers who are exposed to cues that encourage smoking end up smoking more than when their mind is at ease and the same cues are presented. This is the case even when the effects of stress are accounted for (Westling, Mann and Ward, 2006).

But what's really interesting in these studies is that when an environment is designed with cues that encourage virtuous behaviour (messages that discourage smoking or messages that encourage good diets, for example), people become more responsive to them when their mind is working hard on something (Mann and Ward, 2007).

For students, these findings have a number of relevant implications. For example, if you sit down and decide to do your work but your mobile phone is constantly buzzing with notifications and you have flatmates who keep shuffling about, you are more susceptible to being distracted and losing focus.

However, if you go to a library, full of academic texts and other students studying (i.e., virtuous study cues), when you focus on your work you are more likely to be effective in your study habits.

That said, what hampers one student in one environment may not necessarily apply to you. Some students work very well in noisy and active environments while others prefer absolute silence and inactivity. Furthermore, a virtuous cue to one person does not necessarily apply to another. As such, be sure to take note of your personal preferences and have a place to work that is conducive to your academic efforts.

Here are a few words from Ieva, a business psychology PhD student at Aston University, that briefly sum up one way that students deal with their environments:

> 'A PhD requires a lot of concentration. So, while it's good to have a chance to work at home, I find that I need to change environments a lot. I cannot work in one place for a long time. In fact, some places at university are too noisy, so recently, I have tried small office places that are usually rented to entrepreneurs.
>
> For example, a local company had a free trial for a week where I could use some office space. I signed up and found that I was more productive there. I also find that having other people around who are working helps me to be more productive as well.'

Practical Application

When you sit down to work, put your mobile phone away. Close your email application if you are working on a laptop and turn off or mute the TV. Replace these things with items that remind you of what you need to be doing – things such as academic texts, notes and stationery. Is this all a bit extreme? It depends on how easily distracted you are, but such cues can certainly help get your mind in the right state to do your work and not procrastinate.

Optimise your body

'I'll do my work tomorrow when I feel more like it. I'm too tired to start it today.' How many times have you rationalised procrastination with such reasons? Personally, I have lost count of the number of instances where I have used tiredness as an excuse to not get started (although sometimes I cheat by having a coffee).

In some ways, tiredness can be a legitimate reason for putting off our work: around 20 to 30 per cent of students endorse it as a reason for procrastination (Kachgal, Hansen and Nutter, 2001). After a day full of lectures, returning home to then be faced with assigned readings can feel like a chore. Indeed, in Chapter 7 we learnt that our willpower fatigues after we exercise self-control (notably, the effort expended to concentrate in lectures). However, it is also possible to increase our energy levels provided we pay more attention to our bodies. Here are some areas you may consider.

Exercise

One way to boost your general energy, focus and attention is simply to be more active. By pushing your body harder you will enhance both your physical and mental stamina. As explained in Chapter 7, a disciplined exercise regime can also boost self-control abilities.

More interestingly, something as different as vocabulary learning has been shown to be 20 per cent faster in students who exercise intensely before the task than in those who do not (Winter et al., 2007). Other studies have evidenced increased reaction times, better reasoning and working memory amongst physically active people (van Praag, 2009). And in one study, aerobic exercise helped children with ADHD increase their attention span (Pontifex et al., 2012). So, if you are short on energy, attention and focus, try implementing an exercise regime in your life.

Diet

Diet also plays a role in how energised you feel on a day-to-day basis. Ever wonder why you always feel sluggish after ingesting a double cheeseburger with fries? The reason for such fatigue is that your body works harder and takes longer to digest foods high in saturated fats. An overabundance of such foods can leave you feeling tired and fatigued.

On the other hand, dietary deficiencies also pose a risk. In particular, a lack of omega-3 fatty acids has been linked to mental problems such as attention deficit disorder and depression (Gómez-Pinilla, 2008).

With the above in mind, be sure to have a balanced diet. Regular meal intervals (try not to miss breakfast), lots of water (your brain works better when hydrated), a healthy supply of iron-rich foods (they are known to prevent fatigue), and a good mix of starchy foods (wholemeal varieties provide energy more gradually), all go a long way in keeping you attentive and focused throughout the day (NHS, 2013b).

Chronotype

A final consideration is to align your work efforts with your chronotype, an attribute that describes your preference for either mornings or evenings. Sleep researchers identify these two groups of people as larks and owls.

Larks tend to wake up early and are generally more alert and energetic in the morning. (They also go to bed earlier in the evening.) Owls, on the other hand, get up later in the morning, are more alert in the afternoon or evening, and tend to go to bed later (Randler, 2008).

It is important to reflect where on the scale you may sit because if you are a morning person, you can achieve a lot more by doing the harder bits of your work in the morning and leaving the more administrative and easier tasks to the later hours. Likewise, if you an evening person, it would be more productive to do the more challenging parts of your work in the later hours when you are most energised.

All in all, it is important to monitor and optimise your body such that energy, focus and attention are not only maximised, but are also used in an efficient manner. Exercise can help boost energy levels and so can a good diet. But to top it off, be sure to align your work efforts with when your body is most alert and energised.

> **Practical Application**
>
> A student who finds it hard to get the motivation or energy to work on assignments in the evenings (a morning type) might be better off waking up early (say at 6 a.m.) and doing their work at a time when their body is most alert. Of course, this also means that they would have to go to bed early enough so as to get a healthy amount of sleep.

Minimise boredom

As we learnt in Chapter 3, being prone to boredom is linked to impulsive behaviours and procrastination. More specifically, we learnt that boredom is inextricably linked to attention. As a reminder, here are some of the highlights we discussed (they will be used as a guide to how to reduce boredom and increase focus and attention):

1   When we find it hard to pay attention but can't figure out the source of the disruption, we conclude that our inattention must be down to the work being a chore; we therefore rate it to be more boring.

2   During our work, when we daydream and wander off to a nicer place in our minds, the work in the real world begins to pale in comparison. This mind wandering essentially amplifies the contrast and the task in front of us begins to look even more boring than it really is.

3   When we disrupt ourselves (checking Facebook or Twitter every five minutes, for example), we pay less attention to our work and end up not doing as well as we could were we to be fully engaged. We then produce poor work, but instead of attributing this to our lack of focus, we more often than not conclude that it's down to the work being boring.

4   When someone makes us do something against our will, it is more likely to be perceived as boring than when we choose to do it out of our own free will. In the wise words of the comic strip character, Calvin, from *Calvin and Hobbes*, 'It's only work if someone makes you do it!'

5   Also, constantly watching the clock as you work makes time seem longer. And when time drags, the work we are doing begins to seem more boring than it really is. This is in contrast to times where we are fully engaged in our work and are not keeping watch on the clock. In these instances time seems to fly.

With the above in mind (and hopefully you are already beginning to see some possible cures for boredom and how to make a task more engaging), you may consider doing the following as you attempt to get through your university work.

First, if you are finding it hard to concentrate, try to trace and eliminate the distractions that could be thwarting your attention (solves points 1 and 3).

Second, even though daydreaming can be fun, try to do less of it as you work because it will only make your work seem duller (solves point 2).

Third, check the time less frequently, or at least until you finish a specified section of your work (solves point 5). This advice may sound a bit odd at first and requires a bit of willpower, but it helps reduce the feeling of time dragging and keeps you focused.

And finally, make the work your own. Motivation, interest and engagement all thrive when we feel we are acting under our own free will — that is, when we have autonomy (Pink, 2010). So, when faced with a boring assignment, always look for ways you can add your own twist to it (solves point 4).

Practical Application

Let's say a history student has to write an essay on the history of coffee production. The topic may seem boring, until the student realises that they can align it with their love of Starbucks — thus making the work their own. The student could then go on to compare and contrast how coffee production has evolved over the years to what we see on today's high street.

Snapshot Conclusion

- First, once we start our work, the challenge is to persevere and see it through to completion. This can be particularly testing given the number of things that fight for your attention as you try to work.
- Second, our bodies should not be ignored. Exercise and a good diet can help us feel more energetic. Additionally, synchronising our work to when our bodies are most alert can help us achieve more in a limited time.
- Third, increased focus, attention and energy can help us persevere in our work, and one way of doing this is by working in an environment that is conducive to productive behaviours and/or looking for ways to minimise boredom.

9

Goals and Planning

The Procrastination Connection

Without a clear sense of direction and knowing exactly what it is you need to do, it is very easy to freeze in indecisiveness. This chapter, therefore, looks at ways that goals and planning can help you direct your efforts better to avoid falling prey to some of the procrastination pitfalls.

Steady, aim, fire

Life is full of choices; so much so that sometimes it is easy to feel like a deer caught in the headlights. At university we see examples of this when the work set for us is ambiguous, intimidating and too big to start. In these moments we freeze. Unsure of how to proceed, we turn to procrastination.

Even worse, if we are able to start our work but have no sense of direction, or the payoff and sense of achievement is too distant, we end up losing interest and succumbing to disruptive temptations. But there is a way around this – and it is through goals and planning.

Goals help focus the mind to a course of action. If they are challenging (and not impossible!) they can energise you and lead to increased perseverance. Furthermore, goals can inspire you to dig up past knowledge and experiences to help with the successful completion of a task (Locke and Latham, 2002). These are just a few of the reasons why studies have found goal setting to be negatively correlated to procrastination – that is, goal setting can help overcome procrastination (Gröpel and Steel, 2008).

Where does planning fit in? Consider the following example, which puts the two sides of the coin to use:

1 I have a long-term *goal* of completing a presentation on the history of money.
2 I *plan* to achieve this by researching currencies, drafting notes and so forth.

As you can see from the above example, a goal is usually a big-picture achievement. A plan, on the other hand, can be a road map for how to get there.

In this chapter, I will share with you four key ideas that can enhance both your goals and plans in such a way that procrastination is reduced. However, for simplicity's sake I will use the two terms (goals and plans) somewhat interchangeably as the following strategies apply to either.

Be specific

Over 500 research studies tell us that people do better when they have specific, challenging goals than when they have a vague and general intention to just do their best (Seijts and Lotham, 2001). In Chapter 4 we touched on this notion in the context of ambiguous assignments, which lead to increased levels of procrastination. However, the concept also generally extends to how you set goals and plan your work.

Being specific in what you would like to achieve and how you intend to go about it can enhance productivity and performance because such clarity eliminates decision paralysis (e.g., 'what should I write about in this essay?') and provides a vivid benchmark against which effort can be regulated (Schunk, 2001). Another way to put it is this: it is impossible to score without goal posts.

For instance, merely having the aim of completing an essay is nowhere near as effective as having a goal or plan of making six clear arguments for and against a given proposition. In the first situation, you may start your work but then find it hard to complete because there are no clear signposts of progress. In the second situation, however, you are more likely to persist in your efforts because you know that if you make just six points, you will reach the finish line and achieve your personal target.

So try to be specific in the aims, goals and plans that you make regarding your work. Being specific has been shown to help employees be more productive (Locke and Latham, 2002), has helped obese people lose more weight (Bandura and Simon, 1977), and can motivate

Practical Application

Let's say you are a civil engineering student and have an upcoming test on fluid mechanics. Don't just have a large goal of learning the topic. That is, instead of thinking, 'I have to revise fluid mechanics; it's such a big topic!', consider the following three steps:

1 'I will start my revision by mastering the key definitions and fundamentals.
2 I will then look at hydrostatistics and buoyancy in detail.
3 At the end I will quiz myself with 20 questions ...' and so forth.

students to keep to their commitments (Owens, Bowman and Dill, 2008).

In a nutshell, pondering exactly how you intend to complete an assignment can go a long way in remedying the tendency to procrastinate.

Vary learning and performing goals

In goal-setting theory, psychologists distinguish two types of goals: *learning goals* (sometimes referred to as mastery goals) and *performance goals*.

Learning goals emphasise the discovery and acquisition of new skills and knowledge (Seijts and Latham, 2005). There is also usually an emphasis on simply doing one's best.

On the other hand, performance goals emphasise performance against a set benchmark: for example, scoring 60 per cent or more on an exam. Learning goals tend to be broad and free-spirited while performance goals adhere to specific measures of performance.

There is a time and place for both goals to be used before tackling your work. When we already have the necessary knowledge and skills to accomplish a task, performance goals are known to greatly influence effort and persistence. However, when we are yet to acquire the knowledge and skills necessary for a task, such goals can hamper performance.

Motivation researchers Gerard Seijts and Gary Latham (2005) provide the following illustrative example of how best to balance the two types of goals: If you are learning a new sport, say golf, you should first set yourself qualitative goals (e.g., how to hold a club and when to hit the ball) before setting yourself quantitative goals (e.g., a golf score of 95).

Such a strategy is superior since establishing high performance goals too early only sets you up for disappointment that can damage self-confidence. Not only that, instead of your brain focusing on attaining the skills required to do well in a task, it ends up being anxiously preoccupied with meeting some quantitative target.

How does this apply in the student world and how does it tie in with procrastination? Well, starting with learning goals can help you remedy the malady of not knowing where to begin. For example, you need to carry out research to learn what to write about. Therefore, blindly setting yourself a word target of 200 words a day is not as effective as also setting aside some time to research and learn about what you intend to write about.

Likewise, you need to revise and learn your course content before attempting a mock exam. Only after you achieve the aims of learning various topics on your course will the goal of achieving a certain score in an exam be motivating and not discouraging. So, as you plan your work, be sure to set some initial learning goals before setting performance goals.

> ### Practical Application
>
> **A music student who is tasked with composing a piece of music is likely to hit writer's block at some point (this is usually used as an excuse to procrastinate). To overcome this, they could set aside a day to practise scales or to listen to, analyse and be inspired by other pieces of music (learning goals) before setting aside time to write one or two pieces of music (qualitative goals).**

Divide to conquer

The Great Pyramid of Giza, one of the Seven Wonders of the World, stands nearly 50 stories high and would cost billions of pounds to build today. How was it constructed? It's a cliché but you guessed it: one stone at a time. It took the Egyptians over 20 years and tens of thousands of labourers to build the structure. Imagine the amount of vision, planning and persistence that Pharaoh Khufu and his architects had to muster.

Thankfully, our academic work is nowhere near as momentous as the great pyramids. However, we too are better off taking things one block at a time. Why? Because if we start with a lofty goal of, say, getting over 70 per cent in an exam, but then judge ourselves on the results of the first mock exam we take, we are bound to be disappointed. When current performance doesn't match our future ideal, it is easy to lose interest and motivation.

The richer strategy, therefore, is not just to have a goal, but to break it into a subset of smaller steps. It is what four-time Olympic gold medallist swimmer, John Naber, did in his training. His distant goal was to win a gold medal at the Olympics. But to better manage the training process, he set himself the sub-goals (sometimes referred to as proximal goals) of achieving a few hundredths of a second on each training day. Over the course of several months and years, he eventually achieved his goal of winning gold (Seijts and Latham, 2005).

Outside of sports, sub-goals are known to foster rapid self-directed learning, increased self-efficacy, and increased interest in the task at hand (Bandura and Schunk, 1981). You learn faster because sub-goals provide you with more immediate cues about whether your efforts are aligned with what is required to attain your goal (Locke and Latham, 2002); you gain more self-confidence and self-efficacy as you successfully complete each step; and you become more interested in the task as you progressively succeed at it.

In a nutshell, sub-goals shift future feelings of accomplishment to the near term and in doing so remedy some of the failings associated with delayed rewards. Therefore, whenever you are faced with a large, intimidating, task, divide it into more concrete, vivid steps. This will help make your coursework and revision plans more tangible and easier to initiate and persist with, thereby reducing the likelihood of procrastination.

Practical Application

Working on large assignments can be challenging and intimidating unless you break them down and provide yourself with a logical structure that builds up to a whole. The following diagram is an example of the 'divide to conquer' roadmap I used in writing this book. It provided clear mini-goals and made writing the script a lot less intimidating.

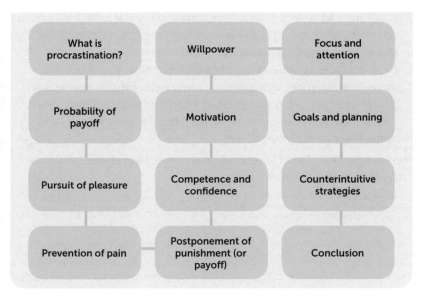

Plan for extra time

Governments, businesses and people in general are often unrealistically optimistic about how long projects take to complete. In Chapter 4 we learnt of this *planning fallacy* and some of its key drivers, namely: (1) being overconfident about our talents, (2) taking credit for lucky breaks while blaming external events for failure, and (3) not planning sufficiently for unexpected and uncontrollable disruptions (Lovallo and Kahneman, 2003).

Underestimating how long something will take and thinking we have all the time in the world diminishes our sense of urgency and can lead to severe bouts of procrastination. Fortunately, the remedies for these faults are hinted at in the above three planning fallacy drivers. Borrowing from Lovallo and Kahneman (2003), here are some ways you can counter the planning fallacy:

☙ When planning your work, don't be overconfident about how quickly you can finish it because you may end up delaying it more than usual. Instead, reflect on how long similar pieces of work took you to complete while ignoring any outliers such as extreme all-nighters. Let this be your base ballpark figure.

꙰ Next, consider possible disruptions that may slow you down. Allow yourself much more time than is actually necessary. By having this 'buffer time' you will guard yourself against unexpected disruptions and, if there aren't any, you can at least finish your work early and either enhance it further or rest.

Here is how Libby Dodd, a second-year criminology student at Durham University, deals with the matter:

> 'The experience during my first year of working until the early hours, having an hour's nap, and running to hand [the coursework] in, knowing full well it wasn't my best piece of work, pushed me into working to a deadline of a few days before it needed handing in.
>
> It doesn't matter whether you think you can bash it out in a couple of hours. You have no control over the flatmate who has just broken up with her boyfriend, or the idiot upstairs setting the fire alarm off. Make sure work comes first; it's a lot less stressful and you can fit in anything else that happens to crop up.'

Fortunately, if you already have the habit of breaking large assignments into small chunks and you use sub-goals often, there is research that indicates you will be less prone to underestimating how long a task will take (Kruger and Evans, 2004). However, always take extra care and allow yourself some breathing space.

Practical Application

If you have an assignment submission date that is two months away, give yourself a tighter deadline and aim to finish the work within one month. You could even use pre-commitment by agreeing with your lecturer or a trusted friend that you will provide them with a near-final draft for early feedback. This will heighten your sense of urgency and provide you with sufficient buffer time should things not go according to plan.

Snapshot Conclusion

- First, your goal is to finish your work on time. So be sure to plan exactly how you intend to achieve this goal. This is because research shows that being specific contributes to higher performance and increased productivity.
- Second, don't just jump into your work. Have learning and discovery goals first before setting yourself the aim of achieving a specific (and perhaps quantitative) performance target.
- Third, don't try to bite off more than you can chew. Break your work down into smaller parts so that it is easier to start and manage.
- And finally, you have less time than you think! Plan for the unexpected and allow yourself more time than is needed. However, you can maintain your sense of urgency by working within a shorter time period.

10

Counterintuitive Strategies

The Procrastination Connection

The last five chapters shared insights on big themes that help address the most common forms of putting things off. However, there are times when you will need to be even more creative in your approach. This closing chapter aims to provide you with examples that can inspire you to think up your own ways of uniquely minimising procrastination.

When all else fails

In the last five chapters we have explored a number of big themes and strategies that can be used to battle procrastination: competence and confidence, motivation, willpower, focus and attention, as well as effective goals and planning. All these themes are certain to help alleviate procrastination and they are a great basis from which to form further strategies.

However, students are unique and what works for one person does not necessarily work for another. In light of this, the current chapter acts as a loose wildcard. That is, below, you will find a few more specific strategies that are not necessarily based on a singular 'big 5' theme but instead draw from various combinations of them.

Moreover, you may find this section of the book particularly helpful in times where the big 5 fail to help. This section of the book may serve as inspiration to help you look for other unique and fun ways of beating procrastination.

Incubation periods

There are times when you can benefit from stepping away from your work and doing what some call 'positive procrastination'. In fact, studies have found that after working hard at something, taking a break from it and doing something completely different can lead to new creative insights.

Einstein, for example, would often turn to music (he played the violin) whenever he hit a ceiling in his work. He found that this was one way of stimulating his subconscious mind to help solve problems he was working on (Shaw, 2003).

So, if you are stuck in your work and feel that you are about to procrastinate, how about stepping away from it and doing something completely different? Perhaps procrastination is only procrastination if the activity you are engaged in does not help you progress in your work. Therefore, it may be OK to do something unrelated, so long as it inspires you to get back to your work with a better mind (reading this book is one example).

Have a busier life

Have you ever noticed students whose lives seem so busy yet they still manage to get a lot done? It could be that there are certain benefits to having a busier life that lead to such students managing their work better and getting more done.

Former derivatives trader turned philosopher, Nassim Taleb, is a proponent of this idea. In a book titled *Antifragile*, he posits:

> If you need something urgently done, give the task to the busiest person (or second busiest) person in the office. Most humans manage to squander their free time, as free time makes them dysfunctional, lazy, and unmotivated − the busier they get, the more active they are at other tasks. (Taleb, 2012)

Perhaps not having much free time helps us in not taking time for granted, which then drives us to make better use of it. So, as strange as it sounds, having a busier student life could be one way of treasuring the time you have and not squandering it on procrastination.

Procrastinate constructively

Many people attest to the power of procrastinating constructively − and indeed it can be useful if the task at hand permits it. Here's how it works: the academic work we have to do usually has many aspects to it and, if broken down, can have a number of mini-tasks that require completion.

So, if you become fed up with one part of your work and are inclined to procrastinate, go ahead and procrastinate. However, do it constructively by picking up another, less tedious, part of your assignment to tackle. Think of it as the equivalent of vacuuming the sitting room when you can't be bothered to do the dishes.

Here is how I applied constructive procrastination when writing this book. One Saturday, after doing a lot of research in the morning, I simply did not have any energy to keep working for the rest of the day. While ideas were still flowing, the drudgery of getting them down in a Word document in meaningful prose was too much for me to bear.

What did I do? Instead of procrastinating by watching a movie or playing computer games, I decided to switch things around. I gave myself the task of transcribing the audio interviews of students I had spoken to on the topic of procrastination.

In sum, when faced with a task that seems unbearable, before giving in to procrastination, look for any parts of the assignment that can be completed with minimal effort. That way, while you may be putting off the harder work, you are at least completing a part of the larger task.

Kitchen timer technique

There is a lot of power to found in a simple kitchen timer. I came across its use after scouring a number of blogs and websites about procrastination. It sounds odd at first, but here is how a simple kitchen utensil can be used to combat procrastination:

1 Decide how long you would like to focus on your work for. Let's say 40 minutes.
2 Set the kitchen timer and focus on your work for the set period.
3 Avoid disruptions during this time and, once the timer runs out, you can rest and return to the urges that may have attempted to disrupt your efforts.

Too simple? Yes. Does it work? Try it for yourself and see. You can use a regular kitchen timer, a stopwatch or a digital app. Anything that allows you to track your work in short bursts of effort can help keep you energised, focused and motivated to finish your assignments.

The scarcity mindset

William Irvine, a professor of philosophy, once wrote: 'someone who thinks he will live forever is more likely to waste his days than someone who fully understands that his days are numbered, and one way to gain this understanding is periodically to contemplate his own death' (Irvine, 2008).

The above philosophical musing may be somewhat heavy-handed and grim, but it highlights an important point. Consider the same quote, but in a lighter, academic context: 'A student who thinks they have all the time in the world to complete their assignments is more likely to waste their time.'

If there were to be one thing I would like you to take away from this book, it would be based on the above notions and would be worded as follows:

Whenever you are assigned a piece of work, understand that your days to the deadline are numbered. Have a scarcity mindset. Appreciate that you do not have all the time in the world and that whatever time you waste, it cannot be recovered.

Periodically contemplating the above will help you tackle procrastination with greater might than you would if time were not of the essence. One way I did this in my work was by having a countdown to an exam pinned up on my bedroom wall, for example.

Snapshot Conclusion

- First, procrastination manifests itself in numerous unique ways. Therefore, some of the catchall strategies provided in earlier chapters are not always effective.
- Second, with the above in mind, it is worth getting your creative juices flowing by exploring other ways you can combat procrastination.
- Third, incubation periods, time constraints via a busy life, and constructive procrastination are just a few other methods for fighting procrastination.
- Fourth, do not rule out simple ideas and strategies that can help you in your efforts to seize the day and get more work done. If something as simple as a kitchen timer can work, who knows what other solutions are right under our noses!
- Fifth and finally, employ a scarcity mindset with your time. Knowing the days you have left are numbered can help boost your sense of urgency and thwart procrastination.

11

Conclusion

Final remarks

Recap

Student procrastination takes many forms, but in the first part of the book we homed in on the four underlying categories of factors that frequently lead to the habit. For ease of memory these were described as the *Four Ps of Procrastination*. In essence, we procrastinate for one of the following reasons:

1 Probability of Payoff – Uncertainty about success.
2 Pursuit of Pleasure – Giving in to tempting disruptions.
3 Prevention of Pain – Avoiding work because it is tough or cumbersome.
4 Postponement of Punishment (or Payoff) – Delayed consequences kill urgency.

To counter the above, I provided a toolset of strategies contained within five key topics:

1 Competence and Confidence – To build the self-belief required for success.
2 Motivation – To find the drive you need to do your work.
3 Willpower – To manage self-control and discipline required for perseverance.
4 Focus and Attention – To maximise energy and concentration.
5 Goals and Planning – To structure your efforts more strategically.

However, we are all unique in the way we experience procrastination and what works for one student may not necessarily work for another. For this reason, a chapter was provided on counterintuitive strategies, the purpose of which was to serve as inspiration for you to generate your own remedies for procrastination (also see Appendix 1, for a 'top 10' list of student tips I was not able to include in earlier parts of the book).

Armed with the above, I am certain you will be able to, at the very least, minimise the amount of procrastination in your student life. Good luck and thank you for taking this journey with me!

Appendices

1 Student Tips Montage

After interviewing dozens of students, I came across a number of tips that I thought would be worth sharing in their original form. Below is a collection of these tips, some of which are from all over the United Kingdom, and some from other parts of the world.

You will note some parallels with the advice offered in earlier parts of the book and, in some places, perhaps even contradictions. This merely shows that the problem of procrastination is not only universal but that you are also better off trying a number of strategies and using what works for you, while discarding what doesn't.

Here is what students had to say when I asked them how they fought procrastination:

Kay Ellis – Pharmacy student, UK
'Timetable it in. If you make time for it, the urge to constantly check your phone or grab a snack goes away.'

Ruvimbo Kuuzabuwe – Creative Writing and Philosophy student, UK
'I trick myself into doing my work: e.g., getting fully dressed as if I'm going out for the day, treating myself to a glass of wine after I've done my work, or telling myself that I can only order an item I want after I've done my assignments.'

Letitia Phillips – Psychology student, UK

'Do not catastrophise! Basically this is when you have an irrational thought that something is far worse than it actually is. In other terms, this simply means: don't exaggerate about how difficult, time-consuming or 'impossible' the work may seem.

Above all, think rationally, you know you have the tools and the time to complete the work and no work set is impossible, so the more you catastrophise, the more likely you are to avoid the work, resulting in procrastination.

If you plan how you're going to approach your workload by setting yourself small, reachable goals/steps, then this may help to rationalise your thinking process, reduce panicking and eliminate procrastination. Optimism is key!

It is said that after a distraction it takes at least 15 minutes to get back to an effective, working mindset, so planning your breaks is crucial as well, to avoid temptation.

A few methods could be to turn off your phone, avoid social networking sites and asking family to help by making you food/drinks (I can't remember how many times I've left my room to make a cup of tea and ended up watching the whole series of *Suits*).

Also, make the work itself that little bit more entertaining by creating a mind-map or poster, as these small activities can help to stimulate neurons in the brain in order to make learning more effective. Nevertheless, this is not to say trap yourself in a dark room with nothing but a textbook.

Positively reinforce yourself (within moderation) by turning on your phone for 15 minutes, walking the dog around the block, learning how to juggle or watching an episode of the *Big Bang Theory* (which only lasts 20 minutes). Above all, don't overindulge!'

Aadhithya Sujith – Mechanical Engineering student, India

'1. Make a list of the things you want to do and categorise it according to the degree of priority and importance.

2. Prepare the routine in such a manner that difficult activities are immediately followed by easy tasks so that the schedule doesn't become hectic.

3. Have time for entertainment and recreational activities like sports.
4. Help others when you can so that they will also help you when you need them.
5. Stop sitting like a rock and start working like a clock!'

Chris Thomas – Psychology student, UK

'Whether you're writing an essay, reading research reports or looking at lectures slides, the ultimate, biggest and most powerful distraction of all is the Internet. A quick trip to look up a reference can lead to a decade of trawling through Facebook photos, falling victim to YouTube or worse ... following Justin Bieber on Twitter! Regardless of which one affects you the most, it is nevertheless a waste of valuable time.

How can we ensure this never happens to us? How can we ensure we remain clearly focused on the task in front of us, without ever having the temptation to web surf again? Yet still remain able to access the sites we need to use for the task, for instance, if we need a reference?

Simple: most people aren't aware that there is technology out there that can help them.

An example of this is a free downloadable program called 'Blue Coat K9 Web Protection'. Although originally designed as an online child protection tool, the program allows you to temporarily block websites of your choice for a set amount of time.

So, if you want to have an intensive hour of work, simply input the sites' URLs and you won't be able to access the sites during the time period you specified. The program is also password protected, so can slow you down in moments of weakness. Pretty useful huh? :)'

Teneika Wilson – Business student, UK

'The best way for me to beat procrastination is to remain focused on my end goals and vision. To do this I create vision boards with a visual of the future I am trying to create. Also, I read inspiring stories on a regular basis about people who have achieved goals and dreams similar to mine.

Having my end visions and goals on my consciousness on a regular basis helps me daily to overcome procrastination.'

Minahil Khan – Engineering student, Pakistan

'I have a '7-minutes mantra'. It is 7 minutes because 7 is my favourite number; you can choose whatever number you like as long as it is within the 3–20 minutes range (the number has to be at least 3 minutes to get focused but also small enough so that you can easily commit). And it hardly requires any effort. Here it is:

Whenever I feel like not studying, I tell myself: 'Just study for 7 minutes, and you're off the hook.' Then I put my timer to 7 minutes and study. By the time it's 7 minutes, I'm done with quite a lot of stuff (because studying for only 7 minutes gets my super-focused mode on) and I always feel like doing just a little more because I can really concentrate a lot at this point.

And that's it! The 7-minutes mantra is easier done than said! Oh and always keep a diary/log, where you can keep track of how many times you were able to beat procrastination this way. You'll feel like a million bucks every time you write it down!'

Jerone Sim – Accountancy student, Singapore

'Firstly, set a feasible target with a deadline in mind. Then decide what little rewards you will give yourself after completing the task and tell a friend or a family member about your goal. This will motivate you to get started on your task earlier, with the reward in mind and the support of a loved one.'

Jade Williams – Psychology and Criminology student, UK

'Well, so far I have not yet fully tackled procrastination, as it's my middle name! To be honest, I rely mostly on being under pressure and doing things last minute. If an assignment was set a month ago, it will get started a week or a couple of days before the due date. Fully knowing in my head that the work will get done, as I never want to miss a due date, I crack on, put on my headphones and start typing till all hours of the night go past.'

Phill Ward, Music student, UK

'Procrastination can happen because we are too intelligent for our own good. When thinking about the upcoming work, our minds will wander through all sorts of scenarios connected with the immensity of the challenge we face. After all, we want to produce nothing less than a top-notch, essay, dissertation or composition!

So the more we think about it, the more we overcomplicate it or worry about the enormity of the work to be done. And then nothing gets done. We're stuck and wasting time that could have been spent simply relaxing!

Also, we want to work at our most efficient, so we put off starting in favour of eating, desk tidying, organising notes, sharpening pencils (actually fun!), etc. Before we know it, we're being texted to go to the pub, and who could turn that down?

The key is to actually START. Never mind getting to a hypothetical mental 'zone' or creating the perfect scenario in which to work – simply MAKE A START. The rest will take care of itself – trust me.

Your first start may even be a false start – 'Oh well, I must get this book from the library first.' Fine. Do that! Or do it when you're next out, and quit worrying. Once you start on a process, your brain will naturally get involved and immersed in that, and that's when you'll get 'in the zone'. But the hard part is starting. Once you begin, anything is possible. Procrastination is nothing but a process that puts you off getting round to doing something.

Also, know when to stop. This can only happen if you've already started, obviously, but know when not to push yourself. Your brain needs time to refresh in order to do its best work. Key ideas can be worked out in sleep, while your brain ticks over. Get started – go – rest. Follow a healthy pattern. Have a tea break. Don't bother making tea before starting, that's big procrastination. Save it for your breaks as a reward.

Make a start! You can do it! Good Luck!'

2 Infographic –The Four Ps of Procrastination

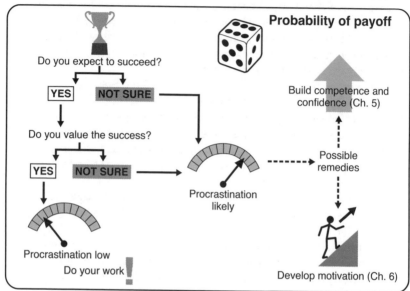

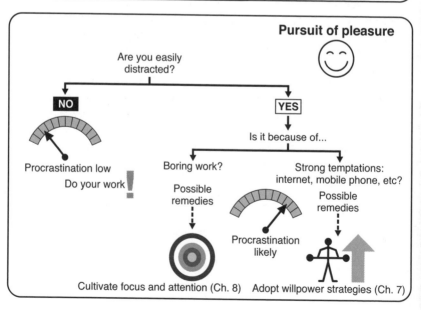

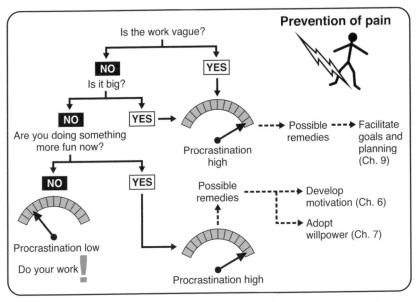

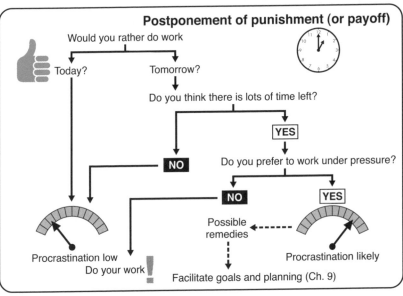

Acknowledgements

Writing a book is never a solo effort and so I would like to extend my gratitude and thanks to everyone at Palgrave Macmillan that helped make this script a reality. In particular, I would like to thank Della Oliver, who has been extremely supportive not only in granting me numerous extensions after I fell prey to the planning fallacy, but also in providing much guidance and advice during the book-writing process.

My family, as ever, are always my biggest fans and I would like to thank them for their continued support in my efforts as an author. I would also like to thank all of my friends for putting up with me being unsociable on occasion, as I powered through various drafts of the book on weekends and late nights.

Last but not least, thank you to all the students who allowed me to interview them for the book. Your insights and experiences contributed greatly in helping me figure out how to stop putting things off.

Bibliography and Further Reading

Adam, T. C., & Epel, E. S. (2007). Stress, eating and the reward system. *Physiology & Behavior*, *91*(4), 449–458.

Adelson, B. (2003). Issues in scientific creativity: Insight, perseverance and personal technique: Profiles of the 2002 Franklin Institute Laureates. *Journal of the Franklin Institute*, *340*(3), 163–189.

Ainslie, G. (1992). *Picoeconomics: The strategic interaction of successive motivational states within the person*. New York: Cambridge University Press.

Ainslie, G. (2010). Procrastination, the basic impulse. In C. Andreou & M. D. White, *The thief of time: Philosophical essays on procrastination* (pp. 11–27). Oxford: Oxford University Press.

Allik, J. (2012). Personality psychology in the first decade of the new millennium: A bibliometric portrait. *European Journal of Personality*, *27*(1), 5–14.

Angeletos, G. M., Laibson, D., Repetto, A., Tobacman, J., & Weinberg, S. (2001). The hyperbolic consumption model: Calibration, simulation, and empirical evaluation. *The Journal of Economic Perspectives*, *15*(3), 47–68.

Ariely, D., Kamenica, E., & Prelec, D. (2008). Man's search for meaning: The case of Legos. *Journal of Economic Behavior & Organization*, *67*(3), 671–677.

Aronson, D. (2009). Cortisol – Its role in stress, inflammation, and indications for diet therapy. Available at: www.todaysdietitian.com/newarchives/111609p38.shtml (accessed 2 May 2013).

Atkinson, J. W. (1957). Motivational determinants of risk-taking behavior. *Psychological Review*, *64*(6p1), 359.

Balkis, M. (2013). Academic procrastination, academic life satisfaction and academic achievement: The mediation role of rational beliefs about studying. *Journal of Cognitive and Behavioral Psychotherapies*, *13*(1), 57–74.

Bandura, A. (1977). Self-efficacy: Toward a unifying theory of behavioral change. *Psychological Review, 84*(2), 191.

Bandura, A. (1997). *Self-efficacy: The exercise of control*. Worth Publishers.

Bandura, A., & Schunk, D. H. (1981). Cultivating competence, self-efficacy, and intrinsic interest through proximal self-motivation. *Journal of Personality and Social Psychology, 41*(3), 586.

Bandura, A., & Simon, K. M. (1977). The role of proximal intentions in self-regulation of refractory behavior. *Cognitive Therapy and Research, 1*(3), 177–193.

Baumeister, R. F., Bratslavsky, E., Muraven, M., & Tice, D. M. (1998). Ego depletion: Is the active self a limited resource? *Journal of Personality and Social Psychology, 74*(5), 1252.

Baumeister, R. F., & Tierney, J. (2011). *Willpower: Rediscovering the greatest human strength*. Penguin.

Bennett, D. (2012). The chocolate machine that can improve your willpower. Available at: www.businessweek.com/articles/2012-05-11/the-chocolate-machine-that-can-improve-your-willpower (accessed 6 January 2013).

Blackler, K. (2011). The effect of adaptive perfectionism, maladaptive perfectionism, and feedback on procrastination behaviour. Unpublished thesis.

Blunt, A. K., & Pychyl, T. A. (2000). Task aversiveness and procrastination: A multi-dimensional approach to task aversiveness across stages of personal projects. *Personality and Individual Differences, 28*(1), 153–167.

Bong, M., & Skaalvik, E. M. (2003). Academic self-concept and self-efficacy: How different are they really? *Educational Psychology Review, 15*(1), 1–40.

Brophy, J. (2008). Developing students' appreciation for what is taught in school. *Educational Psychologist, 43*(3), 132–141.

Buehler, R., Griffin, D., & Ross, M. (1994). Exploring the 'planning fallacy': Why people underestimate their task completion times. *Journal of Personality and Social Psychology, 67*(3), 366.

Burch, K. (2012). Top ten tips for procrastination. *The Independent*. Available at: www.independent.co.uk/student/student-life/top-ten-tips-for-procrastination-7973132.html (accessed 27 May 2013).

Chow, H. P. (2011). Procrastination among undergraduate students: Effects of emotional intelligence, school life, self-evaluation, and self-efficacy. *Alberta Journal of Educational Research, 57*(2), 234–240.

Damrad-Frye, R., & Laird, J. D. (1989). The experience of boredom: The role of the self-perception of attention. *Journal of Personality and Social Psychology, 57*(2), 315.

de Ridder, D. T., Lensvelt-Mulders, G., Finkenauer, C., Stok, F. M., & Baumeister, R. F. (2012). Taking stock of self-control: A meta-analysis of how trait self-control relates to a wide range of behaviors. *Personality and Social Psychology Review, 16*(1), 76–99.

Dewitte, S., & Schouwenburg, H. C. (2002). Procrastination, temptations, and incentives: The struggle between the present and the future in procrastinators and the punctual. *European Journal of Personality, 16*(6), 469–489.

Dohmen, T. J. (2008). Do professionals choke under pressure? *Journal of Economic Behavior & Organization, 65*(3), 636–653.

Duckworth, A. L., Peterson, C., Matthews, M. D., & Kelly, D. R. (2007). Grit: Perseverance and passion for long-term goals. *Journal of Personality and Social Psychology, 92*(6), 1087.

Duckworth, A. L., & Seligman, M. E. (2005). Self-discipline outdoes IQ in predicting academic performance of adolescents. *Psychological Science, 16*(12), 939–944.

Eastwood, J. D., Frischen, A., Fenske, M. J., & Smilek, D. (2012). The unengaged mind defining boredom in terms of attention. *Perspectives on Psychological Science, 7*(5), 482–495.

Ebrecht, M., Hextall, J., Kirtley, L. G., Taylor, A., Dyson, M., & Weinman, J. (2004). Perceived stress and cortisol levels predict speed of wound healing in healthy male adults. *Psychoneuroendocrinology, 29*(6), 798–809.

Eccles J. S., Adler, T. F., Futterman, R., Goff, S. B., Kaczala, C. M., Meece, J. L., & Midgley, C. (1983). Expectancies, values, and academic behaviors. In J. T. Spence (Ed.), *Achievement and achievement motivation* (pp. 75–146). San Francisco: W. H. Freeman.

Eccles, J. S., & Wigfield, A. (2002). Motivational beliefs, values, and goals. *Annual Review of Psychology, 53*(1), 109–132.

Evenden, J. L. (1999). Varieties of impulsivity. *Psychopharmacology, 146*(4), 348–361.

Feltz, D., Short, S., & Sullivan, P. (2008). Self-efficacy in sport: Research and strategies for working with athletes, teams and coaches. *International Journal of Sports Science and Coaching, 3*(2), 293–295.

Ferrari, J. R. (2011). Still procrastinating? One researcher's journey seeking the causes & consequences of chronic procrastination. *Eye on PSI CHI, 15*(2), 18–21.

Ferrari, J. R., Johnson, J. L., & McCown, W. G. (1995). *Procrastination and task avoidance: Theory, research, and treatment.* Springer.

Fisher, C. D. (1993). Boredom at work: A neglected concept. *Human Relations, 46*(3), 395–417.

Fritzsche, B. A., Rapp Young, B., & Hickson, K. C. (2003). Individual differences in academic procrastination tendency and writing success. *Personality and Individual Differences, 35*(7), 1549–1557.

Gómez-Pinilla, F. (2008). Brain foods: The effects of nutrients on brain function. *Nature Reviews Neuroscience, 9*(7), 568–578.

Green, L., & Myerson, J. (2004). A discounting framework for choice with delayed and probabilistic rewards. *Psychological Bulletin, 130*(5), 769.

Gröpel, P., & Steel, P. (2008). A mega-trial investigation of goal setting, interest enhancement, and energy on procrastination. *Personality and Individual Differences, 45*(5), 406–411.

Hagger, M. S., Wood, C., Stiff, C., & Chatzisarantis, N. L. (2010). Ego depletion and the strength model of self-control: A meta-analysis. *Psychological Bulletin, 136*(4), 495.

Haghbin, M., McCaffrey, A., & Pychyl, T. A. (2012). The complexity of the relation between fear of failure and procrastination. *Journal of Rational-Emotive & Cognitive-Behavior Therapy, 30*(4), 249–263.

Inzlicht, M., & Schmeichel, B. J. (2012). What is ego depletion? Toward a mechanistic revision of the resource model of self-control. *Perspectives on Psychological Science, 7*(5), 450–463.

Irvine, W. B. (2008). *A guide to the good life: The ancient art of Stoic joy.* Oxford: Oxford University Press.

Iyengar, S. S., & Lepper, M. R. (2000). When choice is demotivating: Can one desire too much of a good thing? *Journal of Personality and Social Psychology, 79*(6), 995.

Jordet, G., & Hartman, E. (2008). Avoidance motivation and choking under pressure in soccer penalty shootouts. *Journal of Sport & Exercise Psychology*, *30*(4), 450–457.

Kachgal, M. M., Hansen, L. S., & Nutter, K. J. (2001). Academic procrastination prevention/intervention: Strategies and recommendations. *Journal of Developmental Education*, *25*(1), 14–24.

Kahneman, D., & Tversky, A. (1979). Intuitive prediction: Biases and corrective procedures. *Management Science*, *12*, 313–327.

Kehr, F., Hassenzahl, M., Laschke, M., & Diefenbach, S. (2012, May). A transformational product to improve self-control strength: the Chocolate Machine. In *Proceedings of the SIGCHI Conference on Human Factors in Computing Systems* (pp. 689–694). ACM.

Klassen, R. M., Krawchuk, L. L., & Rajani, S. (2008). Academic procrastination of undergraduates: Low self-efficacy to self-regulate predicts higher levels of procrastination. *Contemporary Educational Psychology*, *33*(4), 915–931.

Kruger, J., & Evans, M. (2004). If you don't want to be late, enumerate: Unpacking reduces the planning fallacy. *Journal of Experimental Social Psychology*, *40*(5), 586–598.

Kuther, T. L. (1999). Overcoming procrastination: Getting organized to complete the dissertation. *American Psychological Association of Graduate Students Newsletter*, *11*(3).

Lane, A. M., Devonport, T. J., Milton, K. E., & Williams, L. C. (2003). Self-efficacy and dissertation performance among sport students. *Journal of Hospitality, Leisure, Sports and Tourism Education*, *2*(2), 59–66.

Latham, G. P., & Locke, E. A. (1991). Self-regulation through goal setting. *Organizational Behavior and Human Decision Processes*, *50*(2), 212–247.

Lee, E. (2005). The relationship of motivation and flow experience to academic procrastination in university students. *The Journal of Genetic Psychology*, *166*(1), 5–15.

Linnenbrink, E. A., & Pintrich, P. R. (2002). Motivation as an enabler for academic success. *School Psychology Review*, *31*(3), 313–327.

Locke, E. A., & Latham, G. P. (2002). Building a practically useful theory of goal setting and task motivation: A 35-year odyssey. *American Psychologist*, *57*(9), 705.

London, H., & Monello, L. (1974). Cognitive manipulation of boredom. In H. London & R. E. Nisbett (Eds), *Thought and feeling: Cognitive alteration of feeling states.* Chicago: Aldine-Atherton.

Lovallo, D., & Kahneman, D. (2003). Delusions of success. *Harvard Business Review, 81*(7), 56–63.

MacIntosh, D. (2010). Procrastination, the basic impulse. In C. Andreou & M. D. White, *The thief of time: Philosophical essays on procrastination* (pp. 68–86). Oxford: Oxford University Press.

Mann, T., & Ward, A. (2004). To eat or not to eat: Implications of the attentional myopia model for restrained eaters. *Journal of Abnormal Psychology, 113*(1), 90.

Mann, T., & Ward, A. (2007). Attention, self-control, and health behaviors. *Current Directions in Psychological Science, 16*(5), 280–283.

Margolis, H. (2005). Increasing struggling learners' self-efficacy: What tutors can do and say. *Mentoring & Tutoring: Partnership in Learning, 13*(2), 221–238.

McCrea, S. M., Liberman, N., Trope, Y., & Sherman, S. J. (2008). Construal level and procrastination. *Psychological Science, 19*(12), 1308–1314.

Mill, J. S. (2007). *Utilitarianism, liberty & representative government.* Wildside Press.

Miller, J., Flory, K., Lynam, D., & Leukefeld, C. (2003). A test of the four-factor model of impulsivity-related traits. *Personality and Individual Differences, 34*(8), 1403–1418.

Moore, D. A., & Healy, P. J. (2008). The trouble with overconfidence. *Psychological Review, 115*(2), 502.

Morewedge, C. K., Gray, K., Wegner, D. M., Hassin, R., Ochsner, K., & Trope, Y. (2009). Perish the forethought: Premeditation engenders misperceptions of personal control. *Department of Social and Decision Sciences.* Paper 93.

Myddelton, D. (2007). They meant well: Government project disasters. *Institute of Economic Affairs Monographs, Hobart Paper,* (160).

Neal, D. T., Wood, W., & Quinn, J. M. (2006). Habits – A repeat performance. *Current Directions in Psychological Science, 15*(4), 198–202.

Neumeister, K. L. S. (2004). Understanding the relationship between perfectionism and achievement motivation in gifted college students. *Gifted Child Quarterly, 48*(3), 219–231.

Newport, C. (2012). *So good they can't ignore you: Why skills trump passion in the quest for work you love*. Hachette Digital.

NHS (2013a). *A first steps guide to improving self-esteem and confidence*. Available at: www.firststeps-surrey.nhs.uk/Booklets_Aug13/Self%20 esteem%20&%20confidence%20July%2013.pdf (accessed 25 May 2013).

NHS (2013b). *The energy diet*. Available at: www.nhs.uk/Livewell/tiredness-and-fatigue/Pages/energy-diet.aspx (accessed 24 January 2013).

Oaten, M., & Cheng, K. (2006a). Improved self-control: The benefits of a regular program of academic study. *Basic and Applied Social Psychology*, *28*(1), 1–16.

Oaten, M., & Cheng, K. (2006b). Longitudinal gains in self-regulation from regular physical exercise. *British Journal of Health Psychology*, *11*(4), 717–733.

O'Donoghue, T., & Rabin, M. (1999). Doing it now or later. *American Economic Review*, *89*(1), 103–124.

O'Donoghue, T., & Rabin, M. (2000). The economics of immediate gratification. *Journal of Behavioral Decision Making*, *13*(2), 233–250.

Owens, S. G., Bowman, C. G., & Dill, C. A. (2008). Overcoming procrastination: The effect of implementation intentions. *Journal of Applied Social Psychology*, *38*(2), 366–384.

Partnoy, F. (2012). *Wait: The art and science of delay*. London: Profile Books.

Pink, D. (2010). *Drive: The surprising truth about what motivates us*. Edinburgh: Canongate .

Pontifex, M. B., Saliba, B. J., Raine, L. B., Picchietti, D. L., & Hillman, C. H. (2012). Exercise improves behavioral, neurocognitive, and scholastic performance in children with attention-deficit/hyperactivity disorder. *The Journal of Pediatrics*, *162*(3), 543–551.

Putman, P., Antypa, N., Crysovergi, P., & van der Does, W. A. (2010). Exogenous cortisol acutely influences motivated decision making in healthy young men. *Psychopharmacology*, *208*(2), 257–263.

Pychyl, T. A. (2008). *Just get started*. Available at: www.psychologytoday. com/blog/dont-delay/200803/just-get-started (accessed 19 March 2013).

Pychyl, T. A. (2010). *The procrastinator's digest*. Xlibris.

Pychyl, T. A., & Lavoie, J. A. (2001). Cyberslacking and the procrastination superhighway. *Social Science of Computer Review*, *19*(4), 431–444.

Pychyl, T. A., Lee, J. M., Thibodeau, R., & Blunt, A. (2000). Five days of emotion: An experience sampling study of undergraduate student procrastination. *Journal of Social Behavior & Personality, 15,* 239–254.

Randler, C. (2008). Differences between smokers and nonsmokers in morningness–eveningness. *Social Behavior and Personality: An International Journal, 36*(5), 673–680.

Redden, Joseph P. (2007). Hyperbolic discounting. In R. F. Baumeister and K. D. Vohs (Eds), *Encyclopedia of Social Psychology.* Thousand Oaks, CA: Sage.

Roberti, J. W. (2004). A review of behavioral and biological correlates of sensation seeking. *Journal of Research in Personality, 38*(3), 256–279.

Ryan, R. M., & Deci, E. L. (2000a). Intrinsic and extrinsic motivations: Classic definitions and new directions. *Contemporary Educational Psychology, 25*(1), 54–67.

Ryan, R. M., & Deci, E. L. (2000b). Self-determination theory and the facilitation of intrinsic motivation, social development, and well-being. *American Psychologist, 55*(1), 68.

Sapolsky, R. (2011). *The dopamine project.* Available at: http://dopamineproject.org/2011/07/same-neurochemistry-one-difference-dr-robert-sapolsky-on-dopamine/ (accessed 2 May 2013).

Schunk, D. H. (2001). *Self-regulation through goal setting.* ERIC Clearinghouse on Counseling and Student Service, University of North Carolina at Greensboro. Available at: www.schoolbehavior.com/Files/Schunk.pdf (accessed 21 May 2013).

Schwartz, B. (2009). *The paradox of choice.* HarperCollins.

Seijts, G. H., & Latham, G. P. (2001). The effect of distal learning, outcome, and proximal goals on a moderately complex task. *Journal of Organizational Behavior, 22*(3), 291–307.

Seijts, G. H., & Latham, G. P. (2005). Learning versus performance goals: When should each be used? *The Academy of Management Executive, 19*(1), 124–131.

Senécal, C., Koestner, R., & Vallerand, R. J. (1995). Self-regulation and academic procrastination. *The Journal of Social Psychology, 135*(5), 607–619.

Shaw, G. L. (2003). *Keeping Mozart in mind.* Academic Press.

Solomon, L. J., & Rothblum, E. D. (1984). Academic procrastination: Frequency and cognitive-behavioral correlates. *Journal of Counseling Psychology*, *31*(4), 503.

Steel, P. (2007). The nature of procrastination: A meta-analytic and theoretical review of quintessential self-regulatory failure. *Psychological Bulletin*, *133*(1), 65.

Steel, P. (2012). *The procrastination equation: How to stop putting things off and start getting things done*. London: Pearson Education.

Taleb, N. N. (2012). *Antifragile: Things that gain from disorder*. Random House Digital.

Thakkar, N. (2009). Why procrastinate? An investigation of the root causes behind procrastination. *Lethbridge Undergraduate Research Journal*, *4*(2).

Van den Bos, R., Harteveld, M., & Stoop, H. (2009). Stress and decision-making in humans: Performance is related to cortisol reactivity, albeit differently in men and women. *Psychoneuroendocrinology*, *34*(10), 1449–1458.

van Dinther, M., Dochy, F., & Segers, M. (2011). Factors affecting students' self-efficacy in higher education. *Educational Research Review*, *6*(2), 95–108.

van Praag, H. (2009). Exercise and the brain: Something to chew on. *Trends in Neurosciences*, *32*(5), 283–290.

Vansteenkiste, M., Lens, W., & Deci, E. L. (2006). Intrinsic versus extrinsic goal contents in self-determination theory: Another look at the quality of academic motivation. *Educational Psychologist*, *41*(1), 19–31.

Vansteenkiste, M., Simons, J., Lens, W., Soenens, B., Matos, L., & Lacante, M. (2004). Less is sometimes more: Goal content matters. *Journal of Educational Psychology*, *96*(4), 755.

Vansteenkiste, M., Soenens, B., Verstuyf, J., & Lens, W. (2009). 'What is the usefulness of your schoolwork?' The differential effects of intrinsic and extrinsic goal framing on optimal learning. *Theory and Research in Education*, *7*(2), 155–163.

Vyse, S. A. (2008). *Going broke: Why Americans can't hold on to their money*. Oxford: Oxford University Press.

Westling, E., Mann, T., & Ward, A. (2006). Self-control of smoking: When does narrowed attention help? 1. *Journal of Applied Social Psychology*, *36*(9), 2115–2133.

Whiteside, S. P., & Lynam, D. R. (2001). The five factor model and impulsivity: Using a structural model of personality to understand impulsivity. *Personality and Individual Differences, 30*(4), 669–689.

Wigfield, A. (1994). Expectancy-value theory of achievement motivation: A developmental perspective. *Educational Psychology Review, 6*(1), 49–78.

Wigfield, A., & Eccles, J. S. (2000). Expectancy-value theory of achievement motivation. *Contemporary Educational Psychology, 25*(1), 68–81.

Wilson, B. A., & Nguyen, T. D. (2012). Belonging to tomorrow: An overview of procrastination. *International Journal of Psychological Studies, 4*(1), 211.

Winter, B., Breitenstein, C., Mooren, F. C., Voelker, K., Fobker, M., Lechtermann, A., ... & Knecht, S. (2007). High impact running improves learning. *Neurobiology of Learning and Memory, 87*(4), 597–609.

Yao, M. P. (2009). *An exploration of multidimensional perfectionism, academic self-efficacy, procrastination frequency, and Asian American cultural values in Asian American university students.* Doctoral dissertation, Ohio State University.

York U. (2012). *Procrastination and perfectionism: How students can tame the dangerous duo of drained productivity: York U Research.* Available at: http://news.yorku.ca/2012/09/04/procrastination-and-perfectionism-how-students-can-tame-the-dangerous-duo-of-drained-productivity-york-u-research/ (accessed 26 May 2013).

Zarick, L. M., & Stonebraker, R. (2009). I'll do it tomorrow: The logic of procrastination. *College Teaching, 57*(4), 211–215.

Zellner, D. A., Loaiza, S., Gonzalez, Z., Pita, J., Morales, J., Pecora, D., & Wolf, A. (2006). Food selection changes under stress. *Physiology & Behavior, 87*(4), 789–793.

Zimmerman, B. J. (2000). Self-efficacy: An essential motive to learn. *Contemporary Educational Psychology, 25*(1), 82–91.

Index